# BURIED PHILADELPHIA

## THE CEMETERIES AND BURIAL GROUNDS OF THE CITY OF BROTHERLY LOVE

JENNIFER J. O'DONNELL

AMERICA
THROUGH
TIME

America Through Time®
An imprint of Sutton Publishing Inc
www.through-time.com

First published 2024
Reprinted 2025

Copyright © Jennifer J. O'Donnell 2024, 2025

ISBN 978-1-62545-150-7




Typeset in 10pt on 13 Sabon
Printed and bound in the United States of America

# CONTENTS


About the Author                                                    4

Introduction                                                        5

  1   The Colonists and Their Burial Grounds            9

  2   The Rural Cemetery Movement                       30

  3   New Ground for an Expanding Population             51

  4   The Post Rurals                                   69

  5   The Waning of the Philadelphia Cemetery Era       79

Acknowledgments                                                     95

Bibliography                                                        96

# ABOUT THE AUTHOR

Jennifer O'Donnell is a taphophile from Southeastern Pennsylvania with a love of genealogy and historic preservation. She has volunteered at the previously abandoned Mount Moriah Cemetery in Southwest Philadelphia and Yeadon, Pennsylvania, for over a decade and currently serves as the president of the all-volunteer Friends of Mount Moriah group. Jenn has photographed over 150,000 headstones for findagrave.com and publishes cemetery art photography on Instagram @cems_and_things. She lives with her husband just outside the city limits, has a fondness for overgrown cemeteries, and visits burial grounds everywhere she travels.

# INTRODUCTION

Philadelphia is a wonderful location for cemetery tourism because the city is teeming with burial grounds of varying ages and sizes. For many people, a burial ground does not hold more interest for them than what it is at face value—simply the place you go to bury a loved one and occasionally revisit on anniversaries. The idea of seeking out cemeteries to visit feels like a foreign idea, perhaps even one that seems ghoulish or macabre. There are some occasional explorers who might visit a cemetery for genealogy research or because they are interested in an area's history, but they likely do not consider themselves attracted to cemeteries in any significant way. There are, however, many individuals for whom visiting cemeteries is a pastime or hobby they are drawn to passionately. Some may be processing their own grief, but there are many for whom cemeteries are a place of wonder and exploration. These folks are taphophiles (and coimetromaniacs)—people who enjoy visiting cemeteries and therefore spend quite a bit of their free time in them—and they visit to walk, sightsee amongst the monuments, take in the art and architecture, or just enjoy the peaceful, natural setting. Quite a few taphophiles are enthusiastic about photography, and you'll find plenty of artists capturing all aspects of the cemetery experience in a variety of ways.

When considering the "must-see" cemeteries of Philadelphia, most people only give thought to the Colonial-era burial grounds near Independence Hall. Certainly, a history buff hitting the downtown attractions will peer in the fence to grab a glimpse of Benjamin Franklin's grave at Christ Church or stroll by Old Pine Street or Old Saint Paul's while checking out the Liberty Bell and other historic attractions. Although these Colonial sites are very significant for being among the oldest surviving burial grounds in Philadelphia where some extremely well-known citizens are interred, this photographer chose not to revisit the most written about locations with the exception of Mikveh Israel #1 on Spruce Street and it's South Philly sister site, Mikveh Israel #2, both of which required an appointment to visit.

A more avid cemetery tourist might consider some of Philadelphia's other popular burial grounds, such as the crown jewel rural cemeteries like Laurel Hill East and the Woodlands, the sprawling Cathedral Catholic cemetery, and even Mount Moriah, the previously abandoned and largest cemetery in the city. These cemeteries were established well after the Revolution, but they are well known due to their size, impressive monuments and statuary, and in most cases, the events and recreation opportunities they offer to their local communities. It is not uncommon for residents to visit these places for a concert, tour, or market held on the grounds in the same way they would visit their neighborhood park.

While the more familiar locations are included within the pages here, it became clear after making a list of nearly fifty cemeteries to visit within city limits that there were many more beyond the usual locales deserving of attention. Even more so, as someone who feels quite knowledgeable about Philadelphia's burial grounds, it was a surprise to realize how many cemeteries exist in Philadelphia when you actively go looking for them. They could not all possibly be included in these pages, but a good faith effort was made to be as broad and inclusive as possible beyond the usual suspects in order to offer a glimpse into the decaying beauty of the city's cemeteries.

It was also amazing to realize the sheer vastness of how much land within the city is actually preserved by cemeteries and that in a number of instances, the neighborhood burial ground may be the only green space available to residents. A cemetery property may be the largest continuous area filled with trees, shrubs, and pathways, and as such, they are prime locations to find the city's citizens strolling, jogging, dog walking, or engaging in other types of recreation that have little to do with the location being first and foremost a burial ground. However, if you visit most of these cemeteries, you will find yourself mostly alone amongst the stone structures with, at best, a groundskeeper driving past.

It is also important to note that many of the cemeteries featured here were not part of Philadelphia when they were originally established, but they exist within the city's borders today. As the city of Philadelphia grew, every location that was once merely part of the county became part of the city itself. There are small churchyards nestled within myriad neighborhoods, very old Jewish cemeteries that require special access to visit, the careful landscapes of the Victorian-era burial grounds, and plenty of large acreages with nondescript rows of lookalike headstones. Just like the city itself, no two cemeteries are exactly alike, and they each have hundreds or thousands of stories to tell.

One thing nearly all of Philadelphia's cemeteries have in common is the urban landscape that surrounds the peaceful burial grounds filled with mature trees. Many of these cemeteries were established between the late seventeenth and nineteenth centuries at a time when most of the "city" was still farmland. The oldest cemeteries were near settlement clusters most convenient to the local inhabitants, while later cemeteries took advantage of urban growth near what became Center City to advertise a more rural, pastoral setting on the outskirts. Today, these historic cemeteries are most often completely surrounded by the city, whether by tall skyscrapers or densely clustered residences and businesses. Yet when you're inside any of Philadelphia's cemeteries, you often feel transported through time and can imagine how serene these places were when very little of the dense city surrounded them. They are still peaceful in many ways, despite the hustle and bustle of modern life happening right outside their gates, and it is entirely possible to forget you're in a major East Coast city while exploring the grounds.

Quite a few of Philadelphia's cemeteries are defunct or struggling, but the city can be proud of the number that have made a recovery from periods of distress. Here we will visit a churchyard turned daycare center, bunches of cemeteries where general care and maintenance has dwindled alongside the decrease in monies from new burials or perpetual care funds, and a number of places locked up from the world. It is no wonder that urban cemeteries—especially those in existence for 150 or more years—have grappled with the ability to stay relevant and keep their gates open. Time changes neighborhoods, congregations come and go, families move away from where their ancestors are buried, and preferences evolve about what type of burial (if any) to have. Also, quite simply, ground reserved for burial fills up and eventually even the largest cemeteries will run out of room. All these things create a cluster of financial pressure that makes keeping the property safe and stable a challenge.

Despite this, in Philadelphia's extant cemeteries, we find many hopeful stories of preservation and renewal. If a cemetery is to survive in the city and not face dereliction, it must leverage assets other than new lot sales. While some burial grounds have on-site staff, there are also many Friends groups and other volunteers helping to take care of these properties as room for new burials runs out. Supporters have helped turn many of the city's cemeteries into urban green spaces, arboreta, and places of recreation and learning. The remains of Philadelphia's citizens are juxtaposed against orchards and gardens, art and craft markets, movie nights and concerts, birdwatching, and cemetery tours ranging from the mundane to the macabre. *The Cemeteries and Burial Grounds of the City of Brotherly Love* takes a closer look at hundreds of years of the city's history through the monuments, statuary, architecture, and vistas of the patchwork necropolis contained within its borders.

As you learn about Philadelphia's cemeteries and get a glimpse of the beautiful artifacts found within their walls, perhaps you will consider becoming a cemetery traveler in your own right. Despite some modern sentiments, cemeteries are not creepy and need not be reserved for use only in times of grief. Almost every cemetery featured in this book is open to the public and welcomes visitors. Whether you live close to a cemetery or not, there is certainly one in your community that would benefit greatly from your time and support. After all, the people buried at your local cemetery were instrumental in establishing the community that you live in.

1

# THE COLONISTS AND THEIR BURIAL GROUNDS

There are certainly many burial grounds in the greater Philadelphia area that have completely disappeared throughout time, including sites likely used by the Lenni-Lenape and areas used by early European settlers. There were no structured or reserved burial grounds as the city was laid out, but there was of course still the need to bury the dead. Anyone researching their family history in Philadelphia will quickly learn that places like Machpelah, 6th Street Union, Lafayette, Bethel Burial Ground, Odd Fellows Cemetery, and many more no longer exist, though a surprising number of Colonial-era burial grounds have been preserved and can still be visited today.

When a cemetery was to be closed and the property sold off, there was often a plan put in place to move remains to a new location. It isn't uncommon to find old newspaper articles providing notice of an intended move, but quite often these projects were not completed properly, if at all. In far too many cases, not all of the dearly departed from the original location made it to their new resting place, as evidenced by the continuous issue in the city of finding human remains when new construction projects commence. This does not even take into account what happened to the headstones and markers from the first burial site. Records might not have been kept or they may have been lost or destroyed, so often a topside monument is the only evidence to be found that documents an individual's life. Unfortunately, Philadelphia has seen headstones from defunct cemeteries deposited as riprap under the Betsy Ross Bridge, gravestones destroyed outright, or in some cases intentionally buried right along with the reinterred bodies. There might be a single marker or sign that indicates the new location, but details of each individual are erased.

Philadelphia's Colonial-era cemeteries that do remain often feel a bit locked in time. The city grew up around them, but in many ways the cemetery remained unchanged by the outside world as its purpose was never evolution, but rather consistency as a place of eternal repose. These places hold the history of early American colonists within their hallowed grounds and there is always something new to see or learn when visiting. A cemetery tourist gets to meet history head on–whether their interest lies with the everyday or famous people, the art and architecture, or even the ecology and environment–there is something for everyone to learn about and experience in a cemetery.

A number of Philadelphia's earliest burial places beyond the locations in Old City were once part of surrounding townships and municipalities that were outside of the city limits when they were first established. Prior to the 1850s, areas now considered neighborhoods in the city of Philadelphia were simply part of Philadelphia county: Germantown, Manayunk, Kensington, Roxborough, Kingsessing, Oxford, and many others became wards within the larger city. Philadelphia has remained a city of neighborhoods, and these areas are still locally known by their original names.

The Leverington Cemetery was incorporated in 1857 but is included in this chapter based on evidence that the site was used for burials well before the Revolution. The space that Leverington occupies today was apparently known as "Roxborough Burial Ground" for over 100 years and the property is adjacent to the Roxborough Baptist Cemetery—which at least seems to be a different place, but it is hard to tell where one cemetery ends and the other begins due to the lack of a wall or fence.

The first twelve burial grounds we visit here were all established prior to the American Revolution. When they were founded, it was out of the simple necessity of needing a proper graveyard on consecrated ground. One can picture animals grazing nearby with the hustle and bustle of early industry springing up and the eventual closing in of the city around them. Only Old Pennepack Baptist Church Cemetery, which backs up to the Pennypack Park system, feels somewhat removed from urbanization, but travel a short distance in almost any direction and you'll quickly realize you are still in one of the country's largest metropolitan areas. One wonders what the area residents thought of their smaller towns getting subsumed by Philadelphia and whether anyone worried that the oldest cemeteries would be lost to development. Thankfully, these locations have been preserved, even if they are not generally part of a "must see" cemetery tour of the city. The remaining Colonial-era cemeteries have been protected from development, but often the passage of time and exposure to the elements have caused the gravestones to deteriorate. One does not need to be a taphophile to appreciate the quiet beauty of the decaying markers erected in memory of these departed souls.

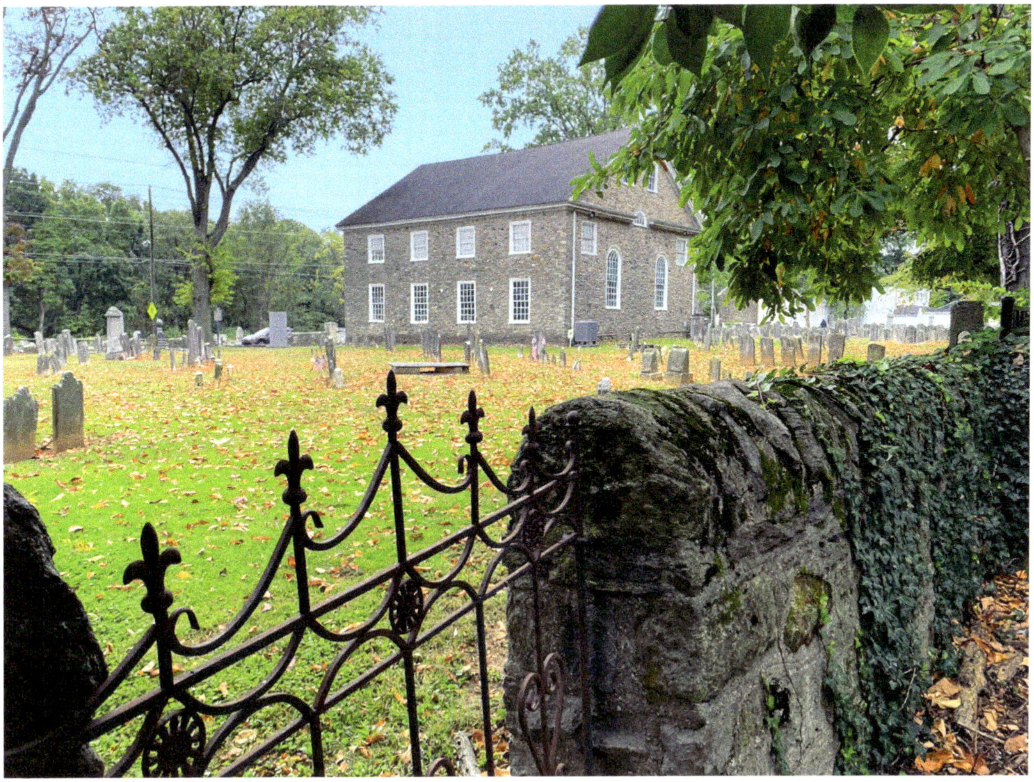

*Above:* Old Pennepack Baptist Church Cemetery had its first burial in 1692, and the quaint churchyard holds well over 1,000 burials of early Welsh and English settlers.

*Right:* An interesting, but nearly unreadable, marker for Reverend John Watts (died 1702) still clearly bears the skull and crossbones and hourglass motif common on seventeenth-century gravestones.

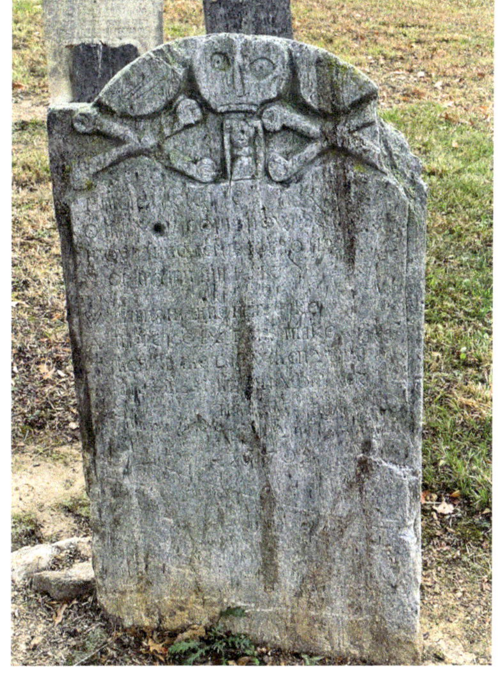

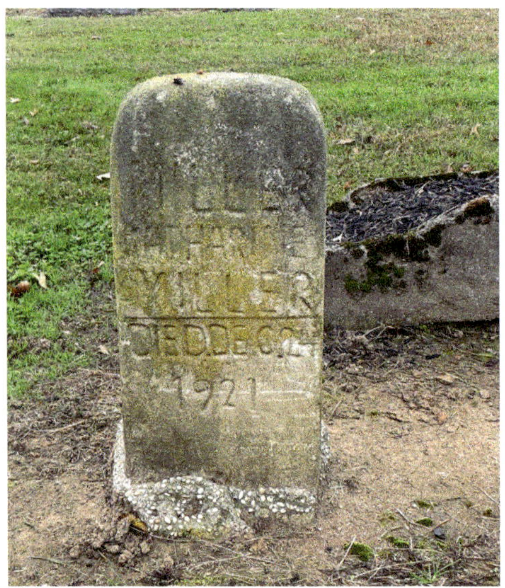

*Left:* Old Pennepack has some wonderful examples of gravestones that were not professionally made, such as this small upright marker for Catharine Miller who died in 1921.

*Below:* The Hood Cemetery, originally known as the Lower Burial Ground, was renamed for William Hood, who donated money for the keyhole-shaped entrance gate and wall. Burials began around 1692 and include a number of Revolutionary War soldiers.

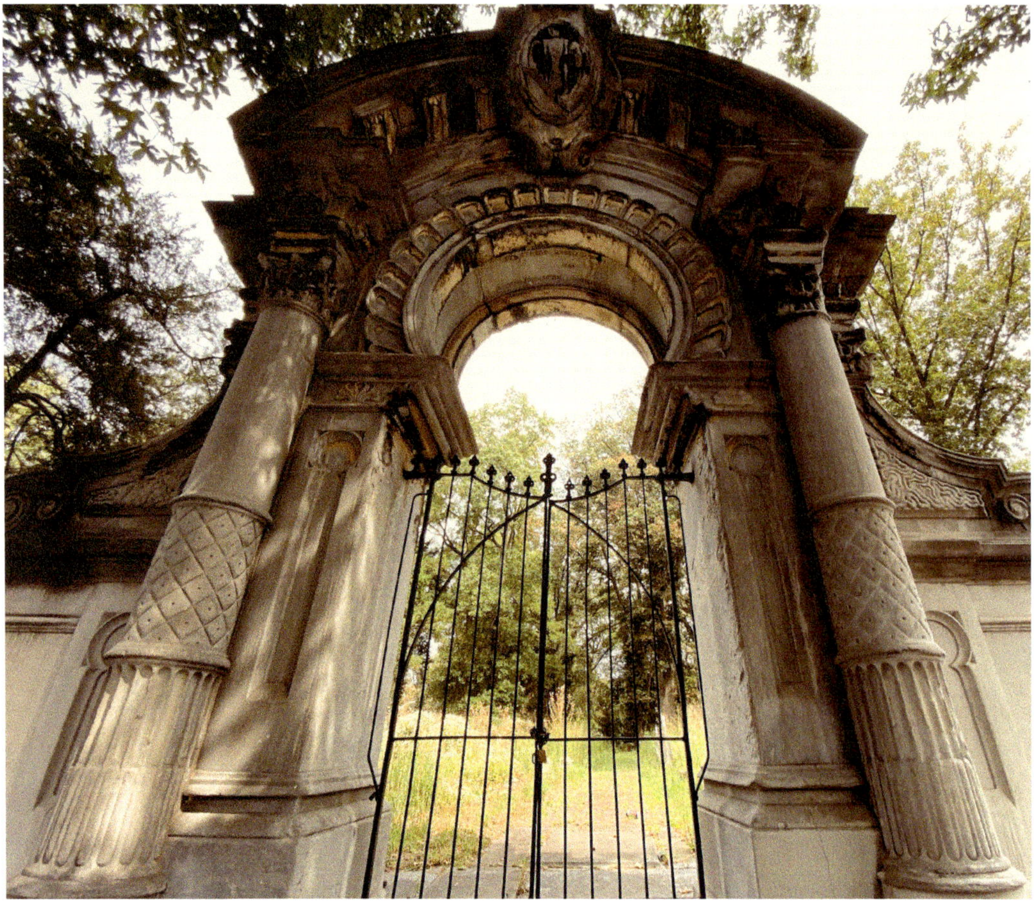

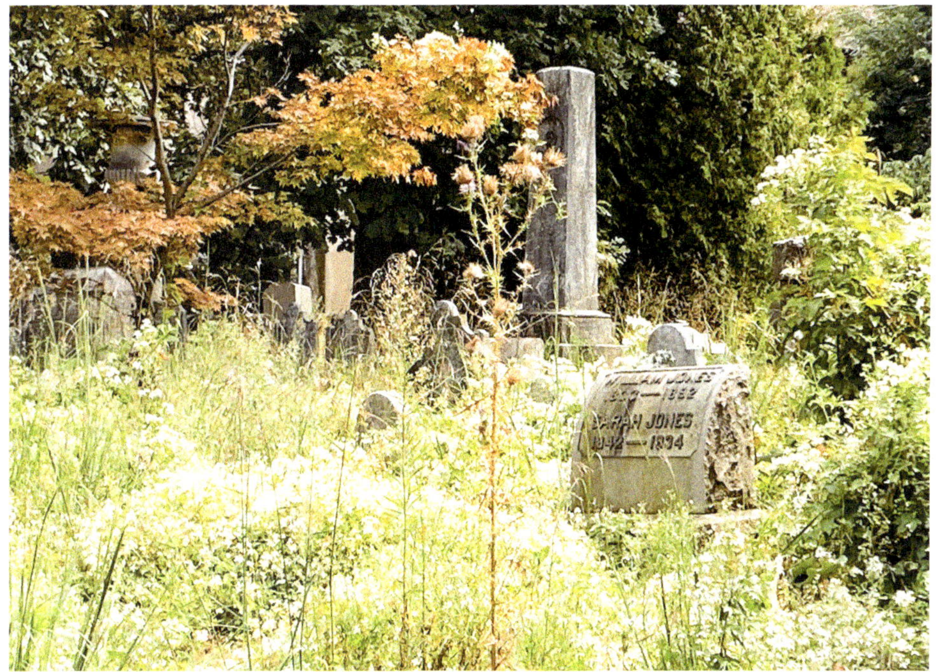

The cemetery is largely inaccessible and could only be viewed from outside the walls. The interior appeared overgrown and unkempt, which is a shame given its historical significance to Philadelphia.

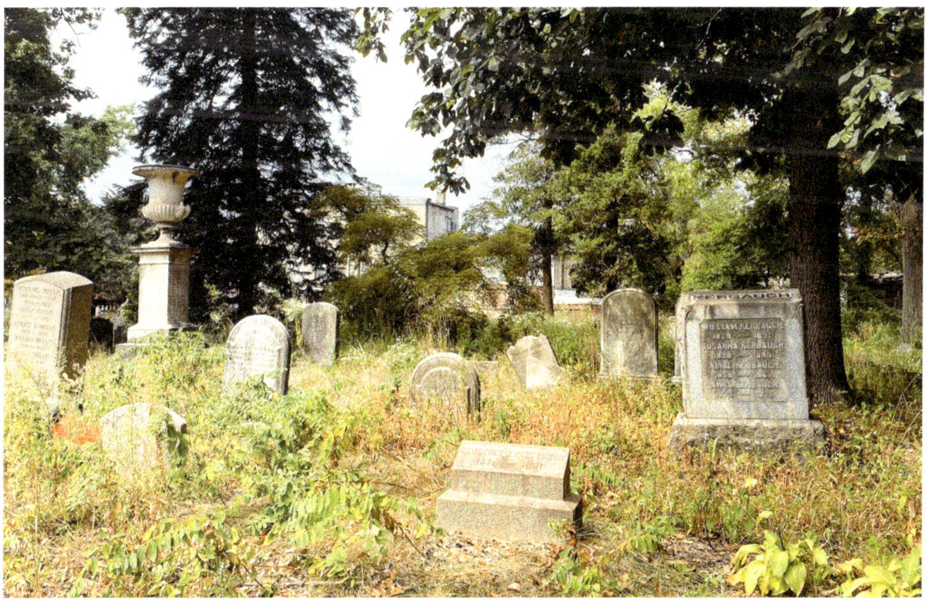

Even from a distance, there's evidence of some striking Colonial-era gravestones, a white bronze monument, and other echoes of Philadelphia's history.

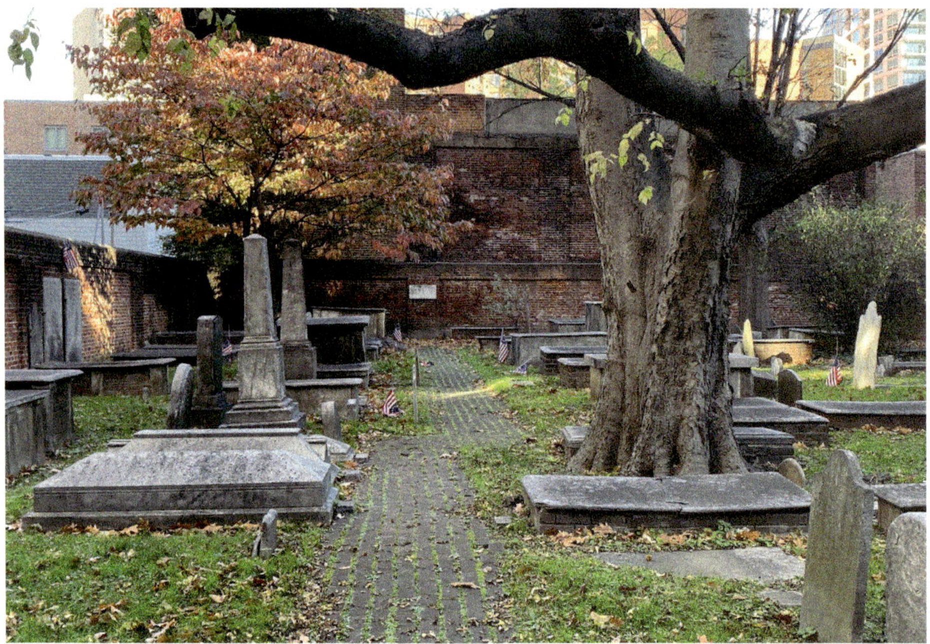

Mikveh Israel, on Spruce Street between 8th & 9th Streets, is the oldest Jewish cemetery in Philadelphia. Many passersby may not realize a cemetery exists here at all, let alone the history just past the iron gate that details the lives and deaths of some of the earliest Jewish settlers in the city.

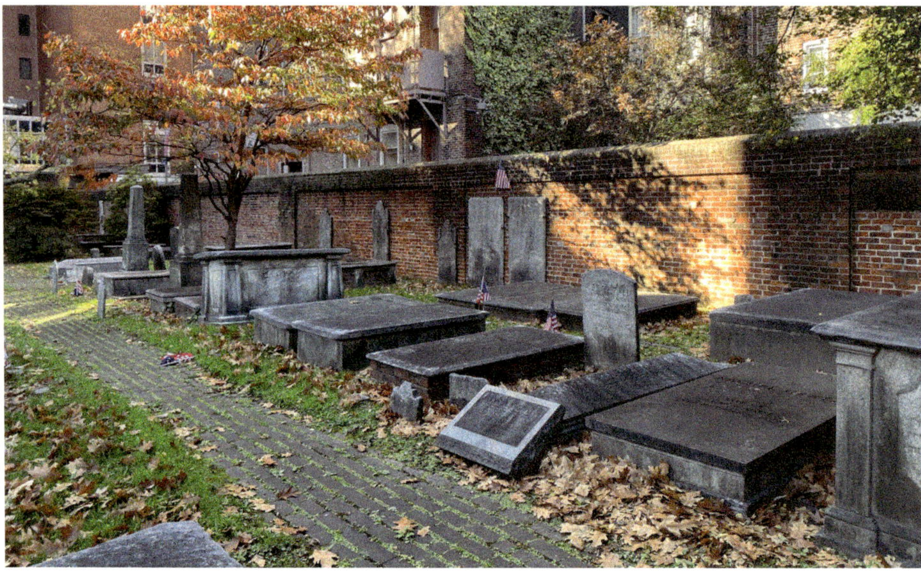

Dating to 1740, the graveyard is enclosed by an early nineteenth-century brick wall and surrounded by tall buildings. There is a unique array of monuments, such as table graves, Colonial-style upright monuments, and more modern replacement stones.

*Right:* There are many markers affixed to the walls, although it's not clear whether this was original or a conservation effort.

*Below:* Even under the best conditions, gravestones don't last forever. Mikveh Israel's headstones have sunk into the ground, been battered by the weather, and cracked or crumbled due to age and external forces.

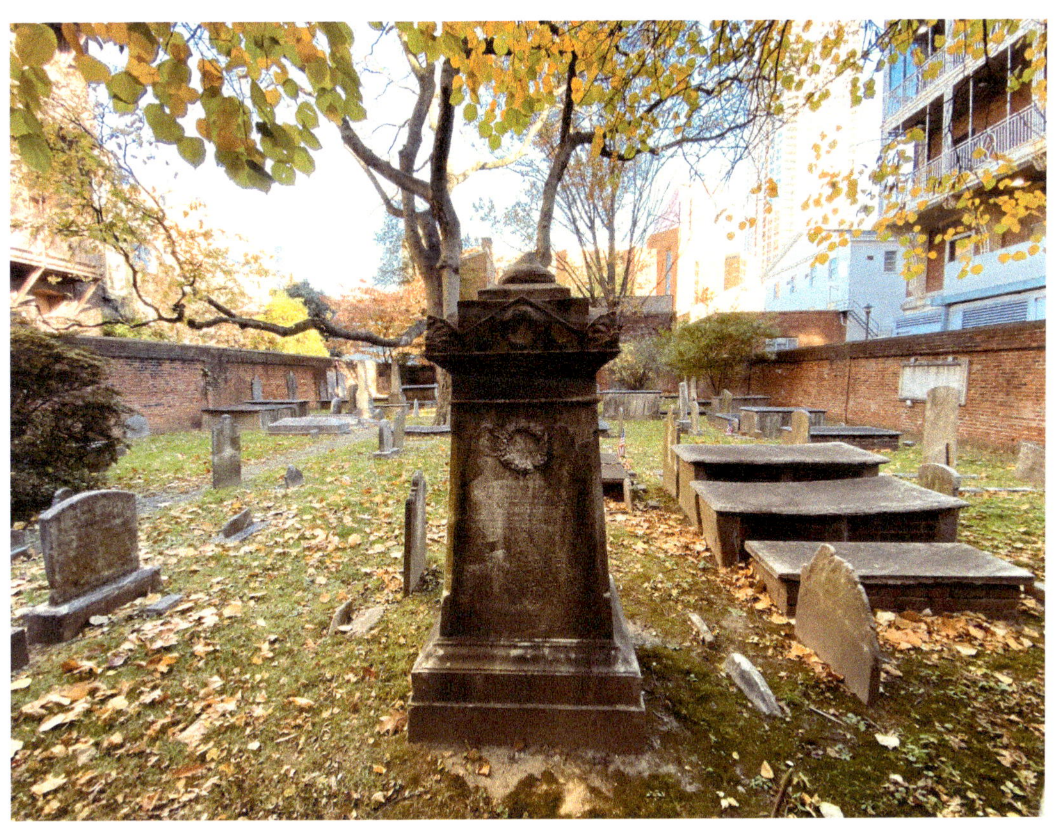

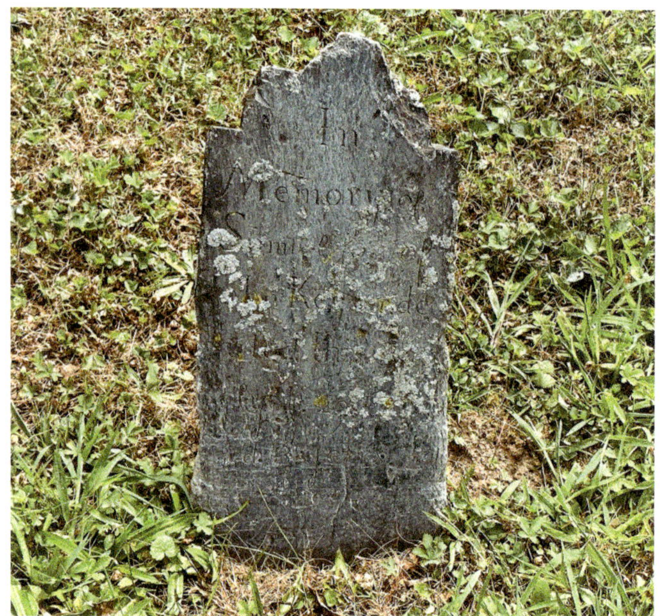

The Germantown Mennonite Meetinghouse and its tiny burial ground were established in the 1700s and contain the remains of the first German and Mennonite settlers in the colonies. The headstone for thirteen-year-old Samuel Keyser, who died in 1773, is one of the few original, legible markers.

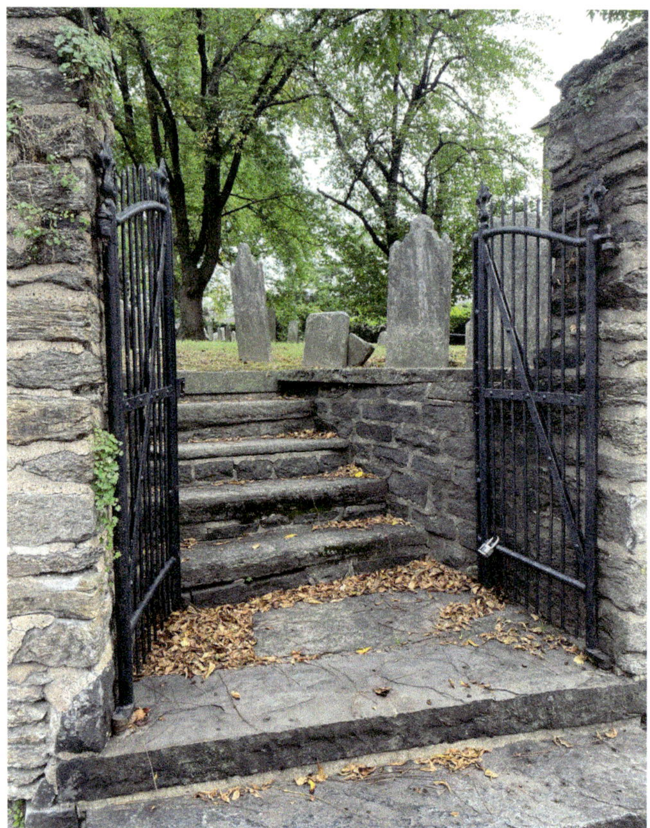

Germantown is also home to the Upper Burial Ground, which was established in the late 1690s. Intended as a place for people of all religions, the cemetery sits a few steps above street level and contains the remains of nearly sixty Revolutionary soldiers who fought at the Battle of Germantown.

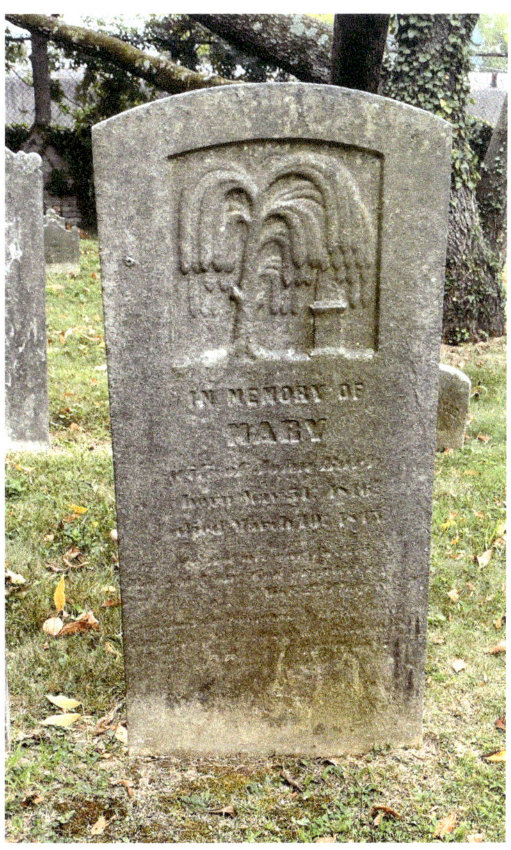

Many of the oldest markers have faded over time, and with no records kept before the mid-1700s, there is little evidence of all individuals buried here. Despite the lack of documentation, the markers are mostly presented in neat, orderly rows and one of the oldest readable stones is from 1716.

The weeping willow tree carved on Mary's gravestone was a popular motif in the early 1800s.

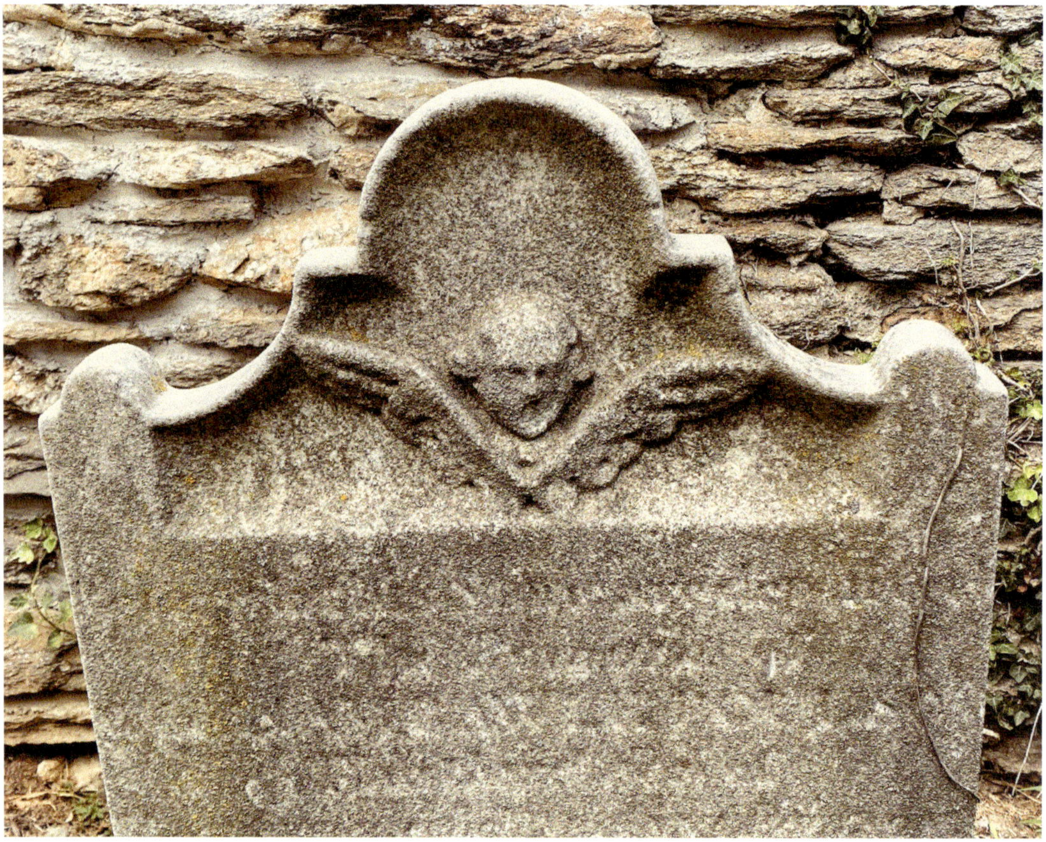

*Above:* Although this gravestone is illegible, the winged cherub at the top is still visible. The cherub gradually replaced the skull engravings seen on earlier markers.

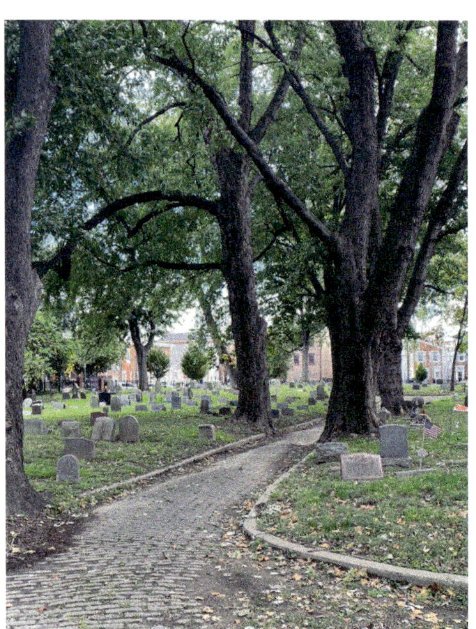

*Left:* The Kensington Burial Ground, known locally as Palmer Cemetery, was established by English settler Anthony Palmer for his family and was turned into a community cemetery after his death in 1749. The cobblestone pathways and mature trees make this a popular spot for local residents to walk and enjoy the peaceful grounds.

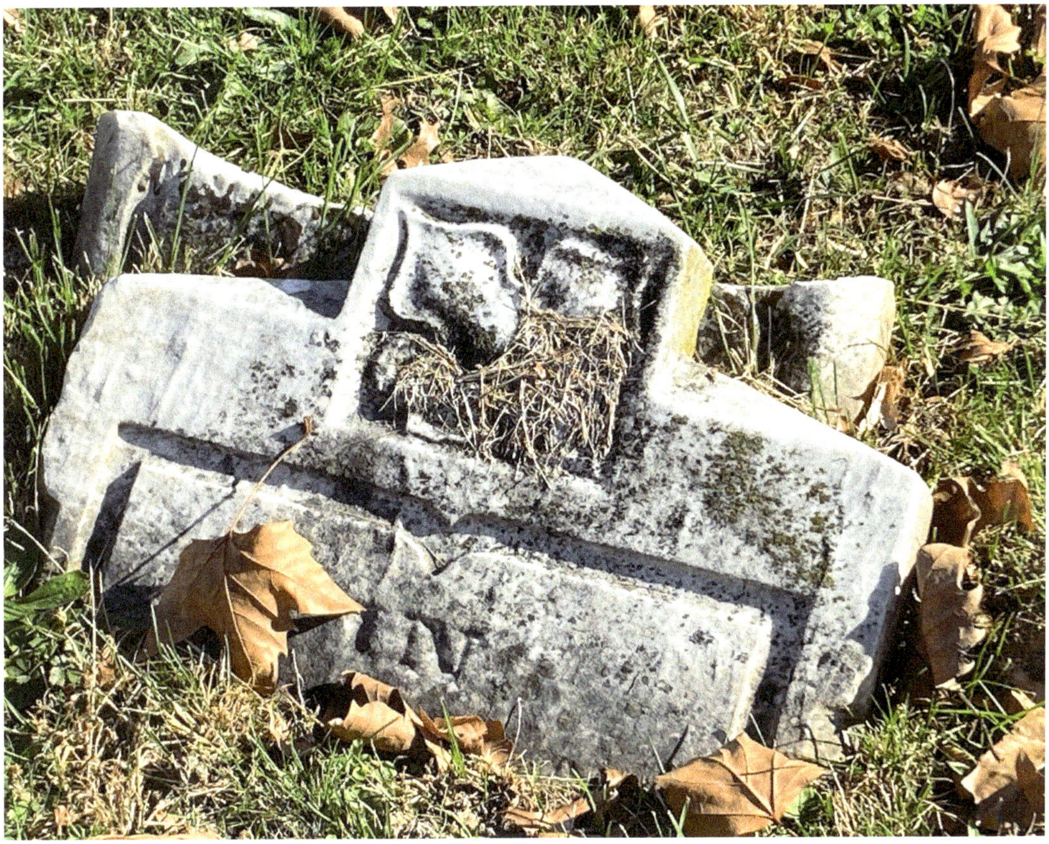

*Above:* Palmer contains the remains of many of Kensington—now the Fishtown neighborhood's—early settlers and their families. Actual burial numbers are not known, but estimates range from 40,000-50,000 interments.

*Right:* The cemetery is still active today, as evidenced by modern markers and trinkets abutting much older gravestones. Like a number of Philadelphia's burial grounds, the care and maintenance of the graveyard relies on donations and volunteers.

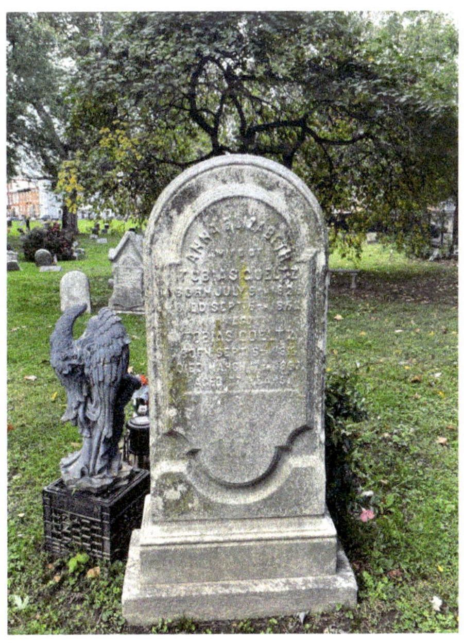

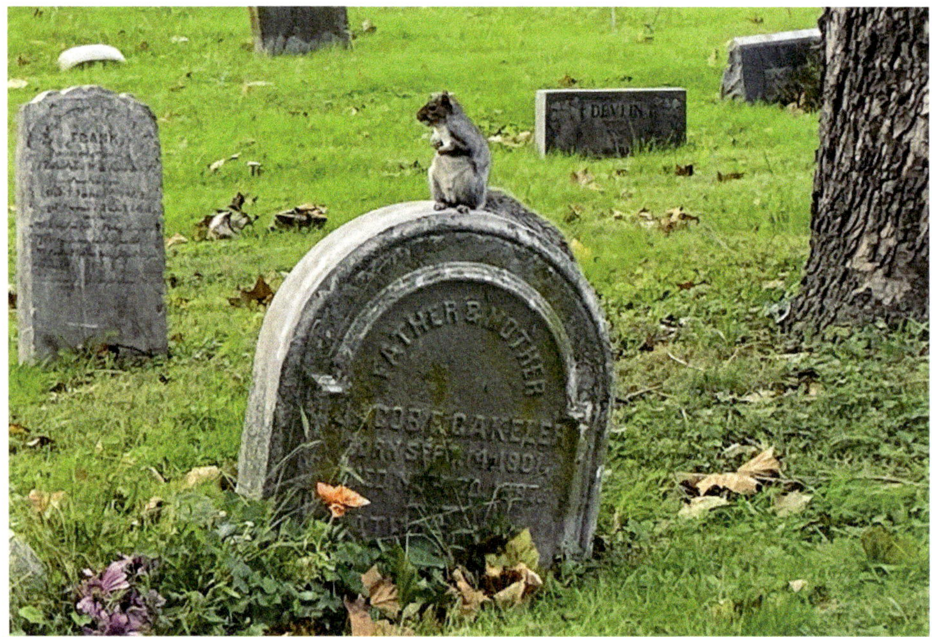

City cemeteries offer habitat for local wildlife, from squirrels and chipmunks to groundhogs and birds.

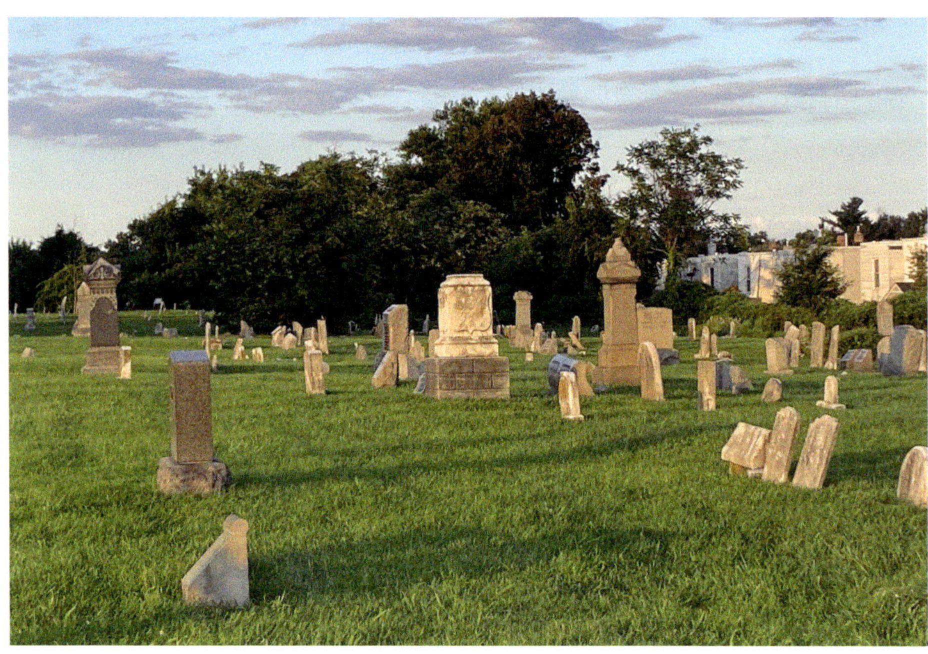

The Roxborough Baptist Church Cemetery sits adjacent to—and seems commingled with— Leverington Cemetery. Burials began around 1744 for the Levering family and at some point, became associated with the Roxborough Baptist Church that still stands in front of the cemetery.

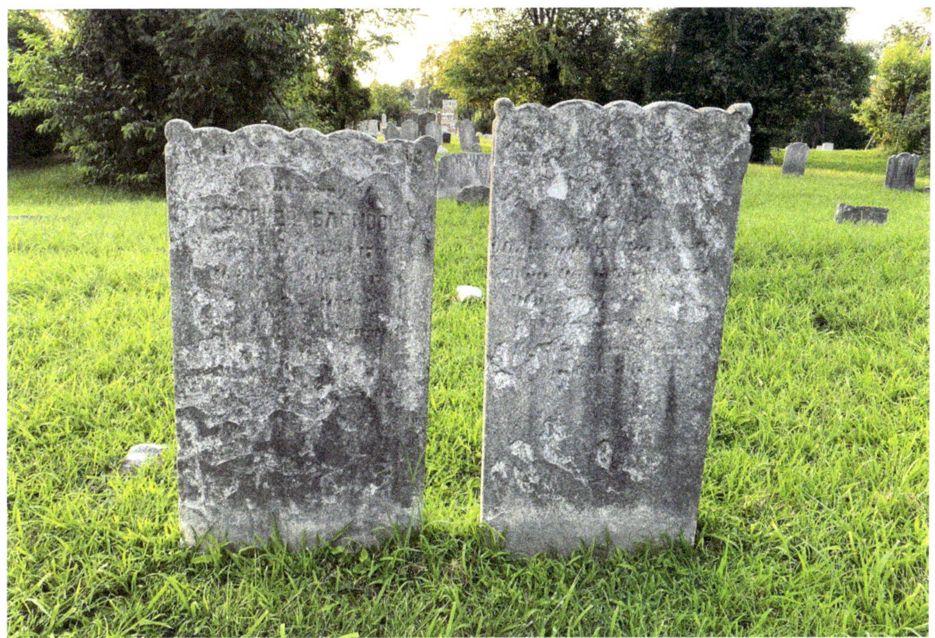

Many of the beautiful monuments at Roxborough Baptist are weathered and unreadable, but they stand a silent legacy to these early Northwest Philadelphia residents.

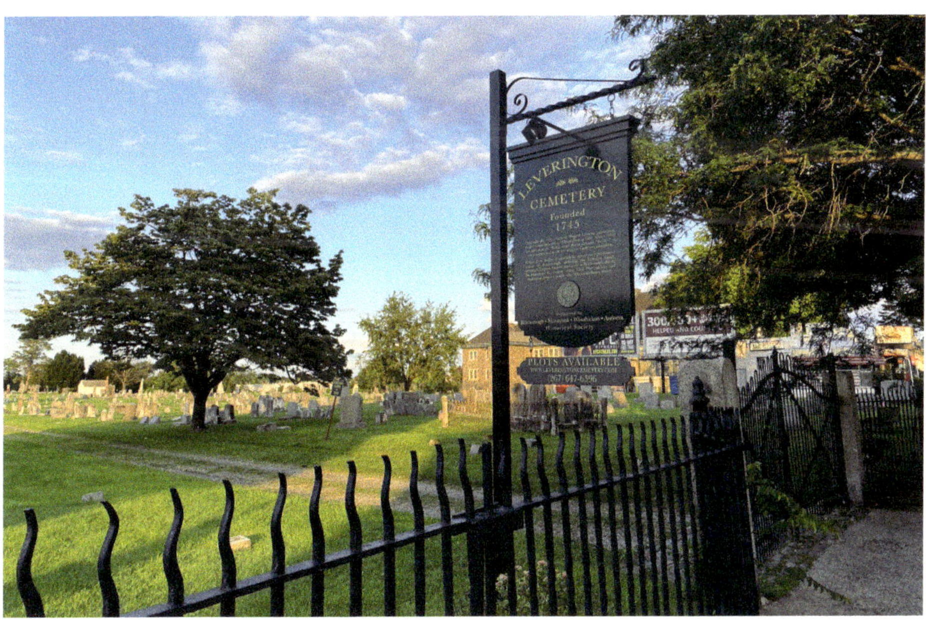

It's hard to tell where Leverington Cemetery and the adjacent Roxborough Baptist Church Cemetery begin and end due to the lack of any fencing in between. Although used as a burial ground for over 100 years, the current iteration of the cemetery was established in 1857 and is non-denominational.

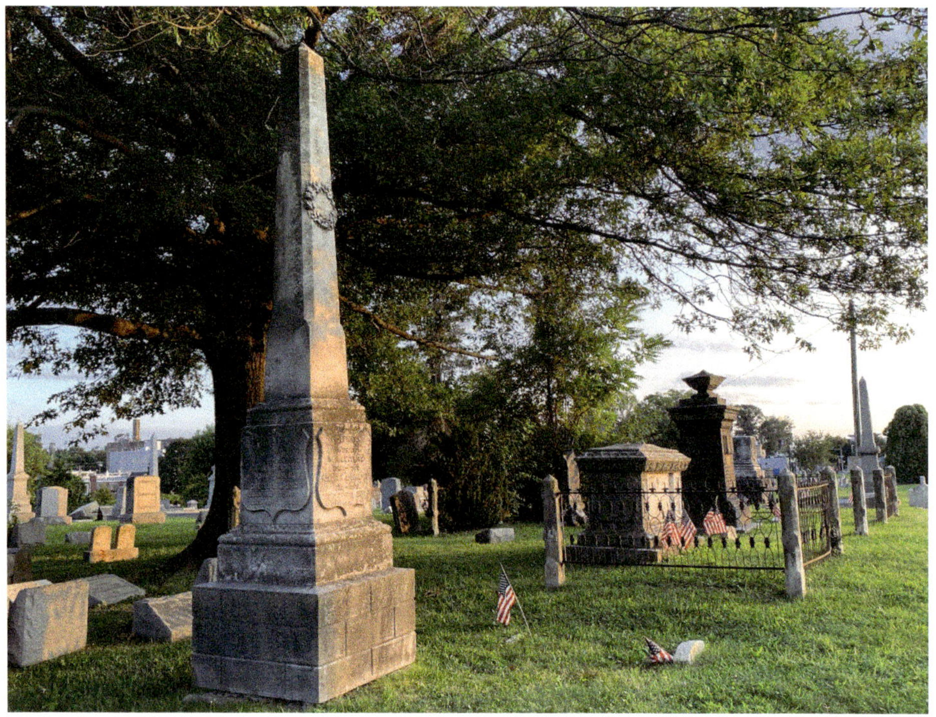

There is remaining evidence of monuments and decorations that were likely quite grand when first made, including some plots that still retain part of their original iron fencing.

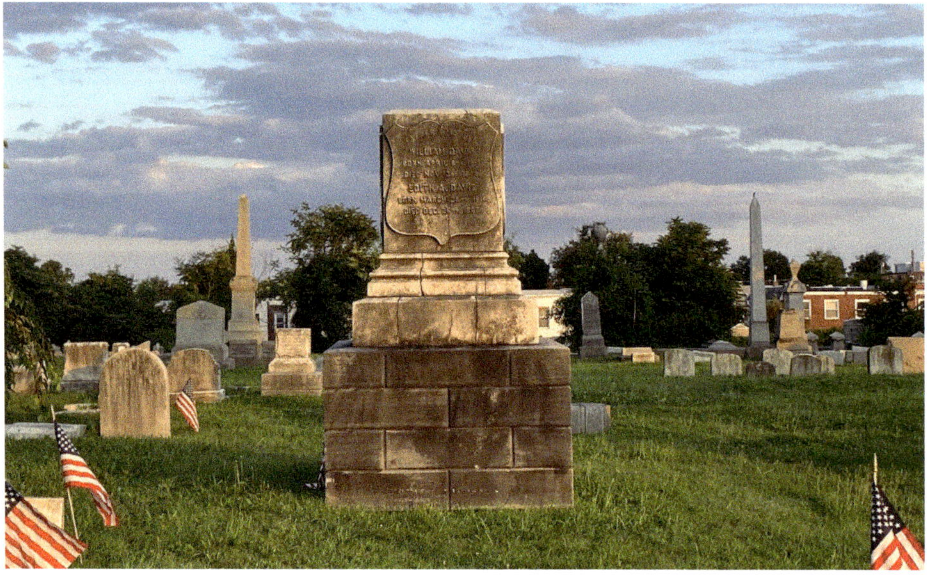

Leverington is still open to new burials, although interments seem to be infrequent. The oldest sections of the cemetery display a wide variety of monument styles and there appear to be many unmarked graves.

*Right:* Similar to many older cemeteries, the lack of aggressive monument preservation has led to many toppled or uneven headstones. Still others have simply faded over time due to the style of stone and exposure to the extreme heat and cold of the greater Philadelphia region.

*Below:* This tree stump tombstone with a cross and flower embellishments likely cost a significant amount in 1898 when Catharine Hagerty died.

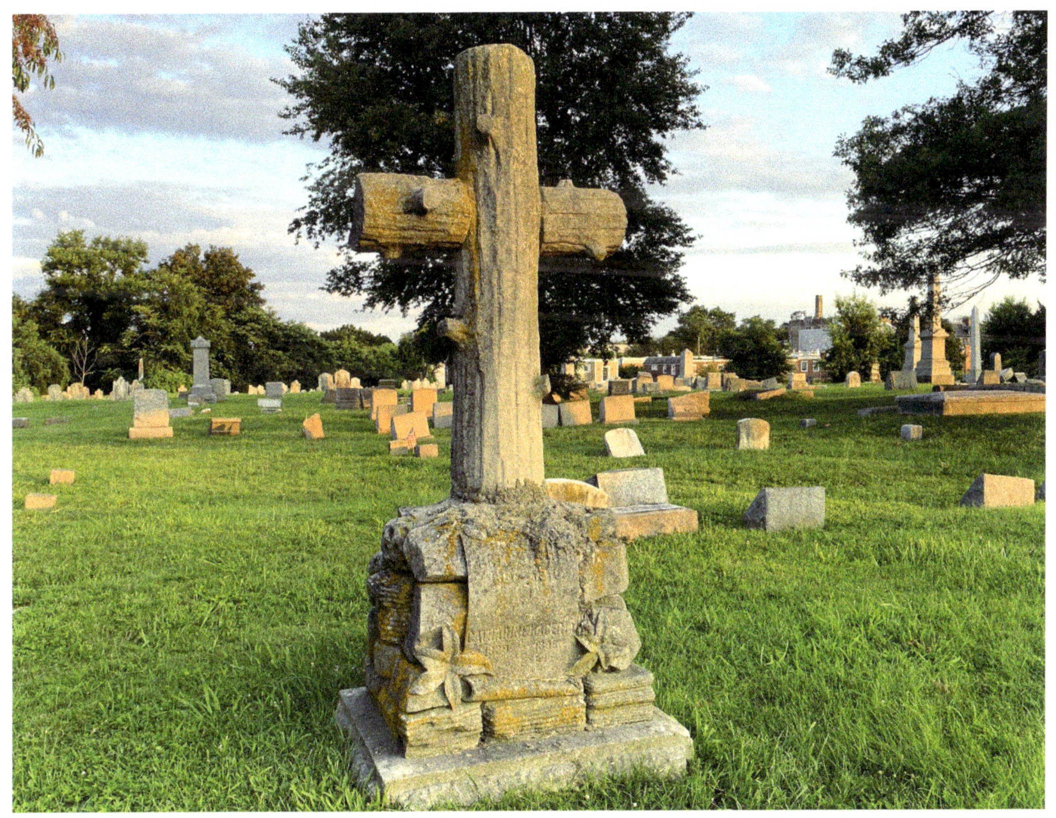

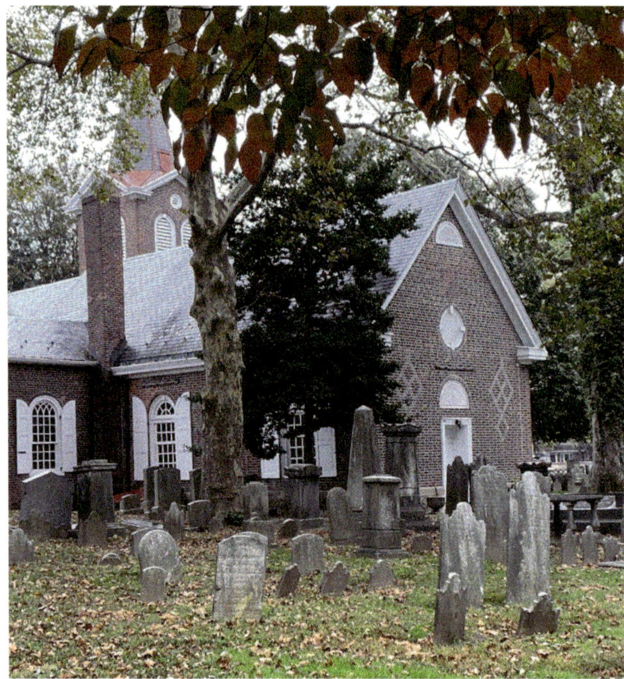

The red brick Trinity Episcopal Church in the Oxford section of Philadelphia dates back to 1711.

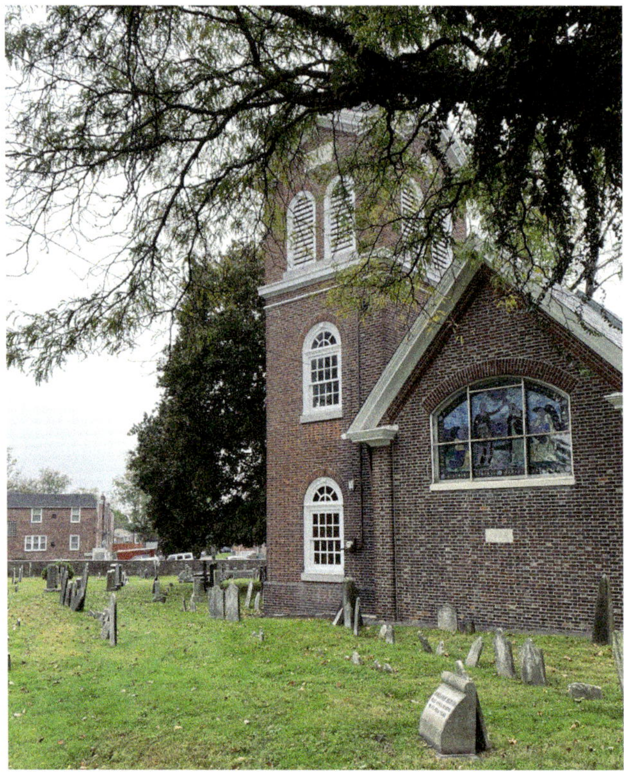

Many of the oldest graves are clustered very close to the church building on all sides.

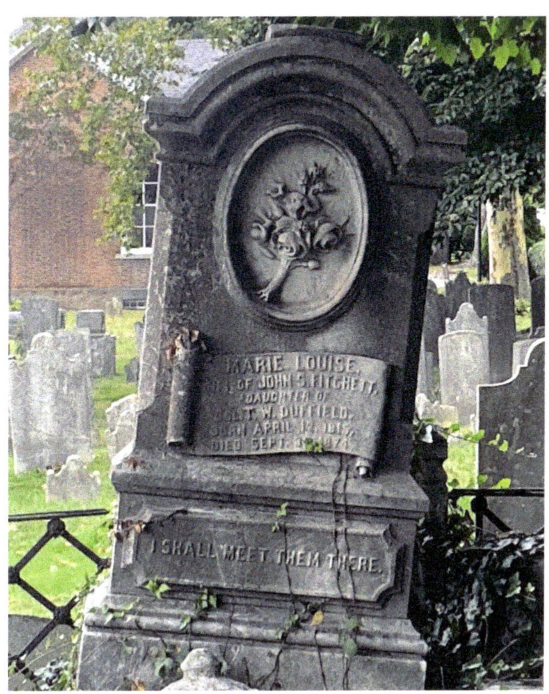

*Right:* Inside a fenced family plot, there is a tilting but beautiful gravestone for Marie Louise Fitchett. The bouquet of flowers, scrolled inscription, and epitaph, "I shall meet them there," is a great example of mid-Victorian-era headstone sensibilities.

*Below:* The Episcopal Saint James of Kingsessing churchyard had its first burial prior to the Revolutionary War. Many of the area's Swedish settlers worshiped here during the time when the area was mostly farmland.

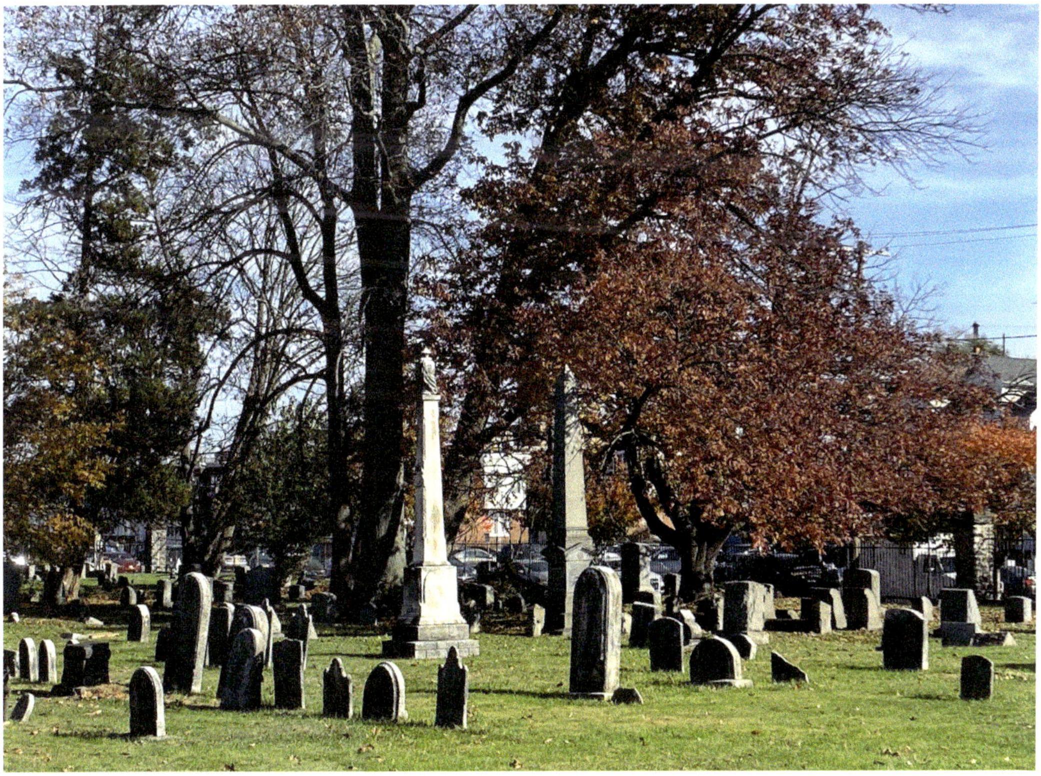

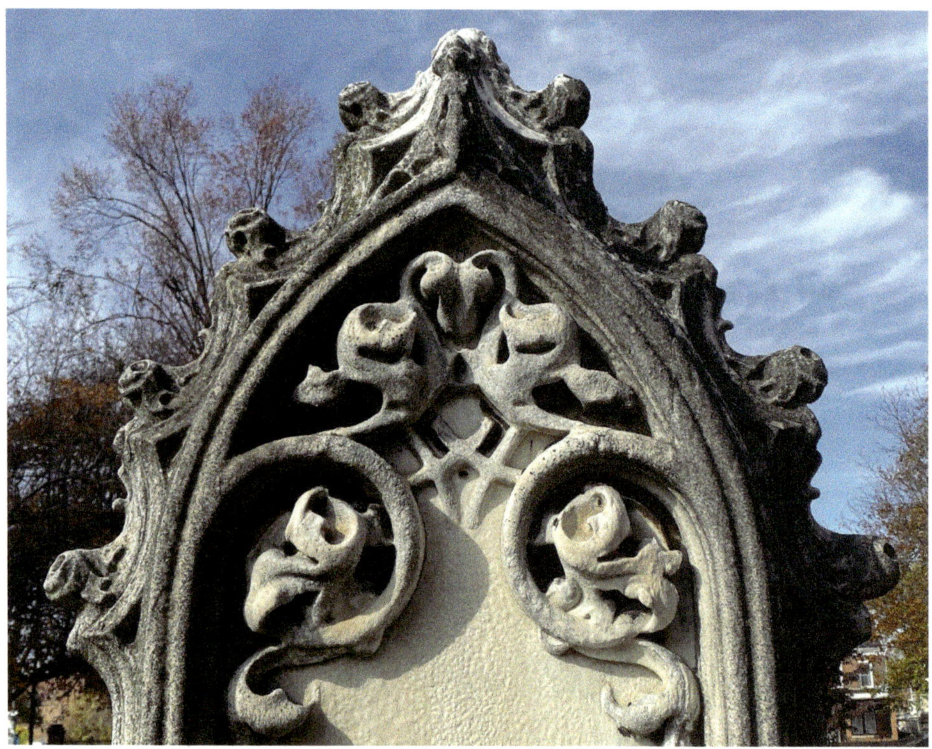

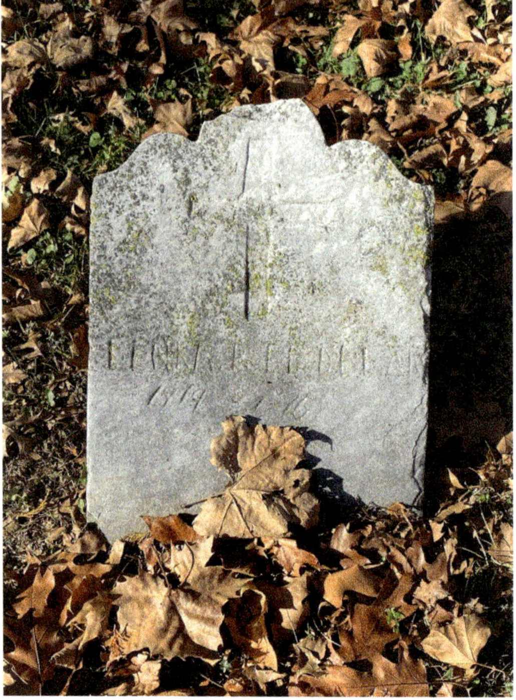

*Above:* The burial ground still appears active, although many of the older gravestones are in disrepair.

*Left:* Many homemade markers have not withstood the test of time, although these are perhaps some of the more endearing gravestones since it was most likely produced by a loved one.

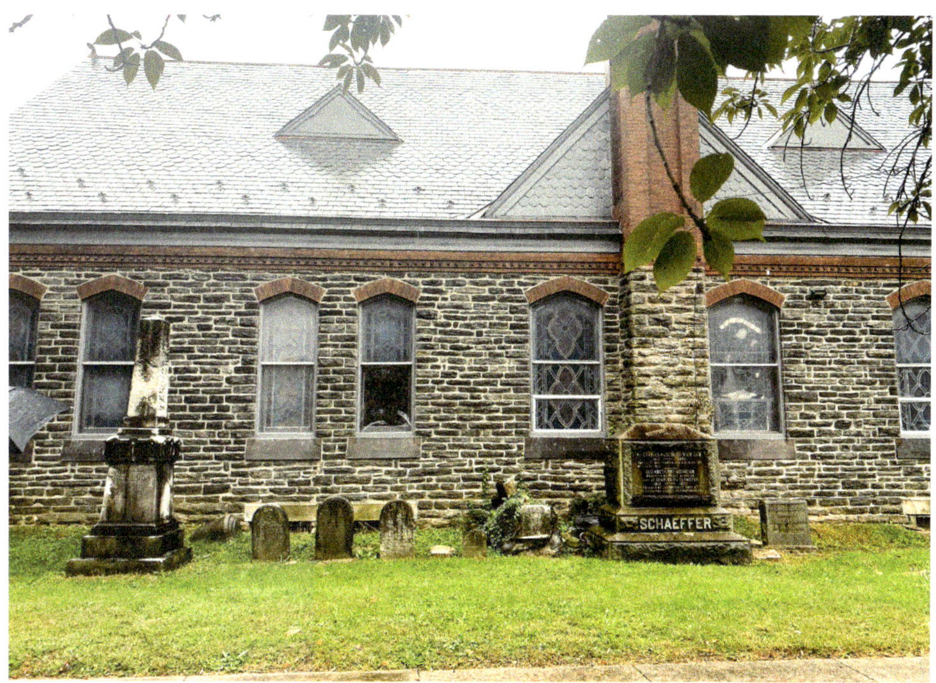

Saint Michael's Lutheran Churchyard in the Mt. Airy section of Philadelphia was active from at least the late 1720s until it closed in 2016. The church itself went through a number of iterations over the years, which may explain why a number of graves appear to be very close to the building.

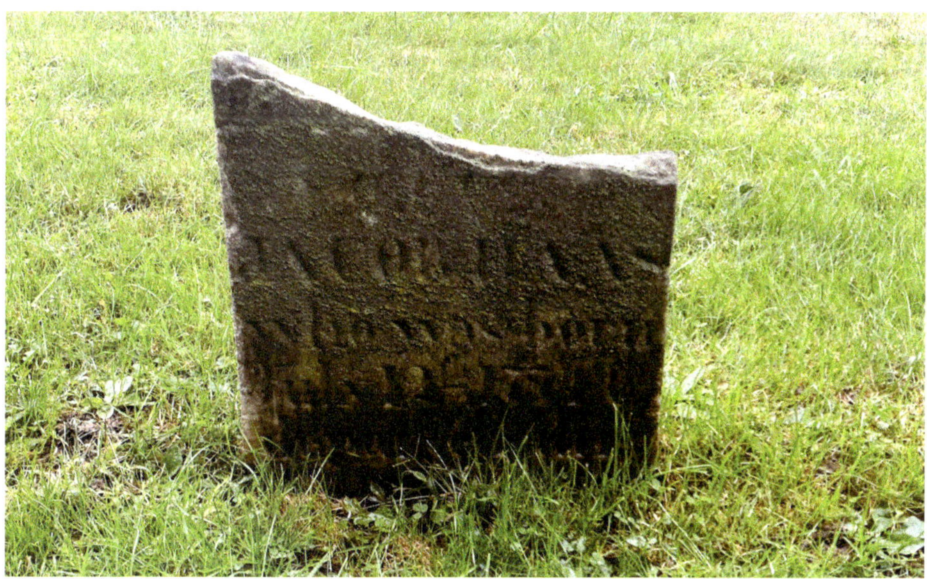

Like so many of Philadelphia's oldest burial locations, many of the markers are broken and weathered.

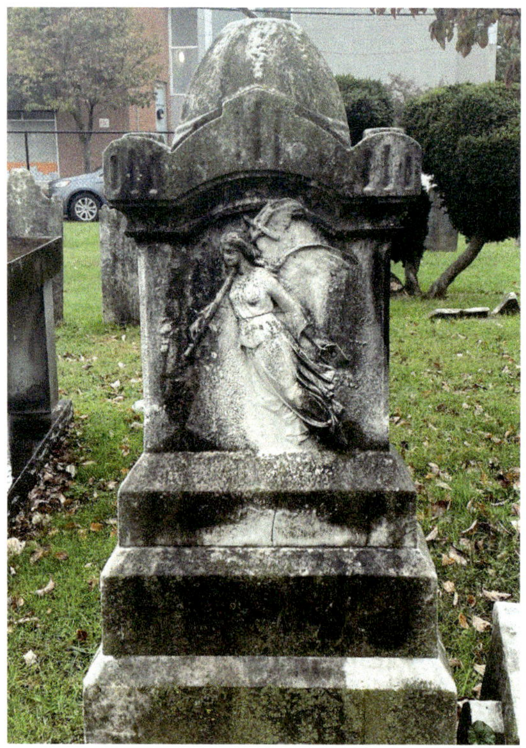

Although the inscription on this marker has long since worn away, the angel motif at the top is still quite striking.

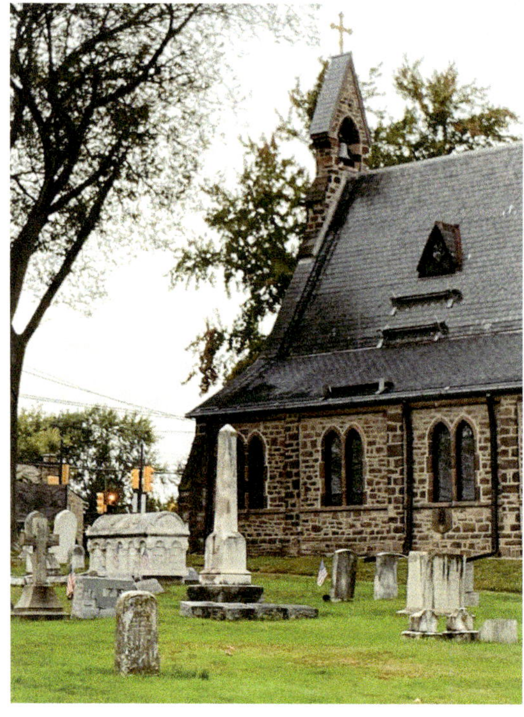

All Saints Episcopal Church in the Torresdale section of Philadelphia first held services in 1772. The current church building was completed around 1855.

*Right:* The churchyard contains a wide variety of gravestone styles, from ornate crosses with climbing English ivy to the simple marker for Mary Toy (1813-1903).

*Below:* This large, sarcophagus-style monument for Sallie Myers who died in 1887 at just twenty years old is a lasting tribute engraved with " … that which thou sowest is not quickened, except it die … "

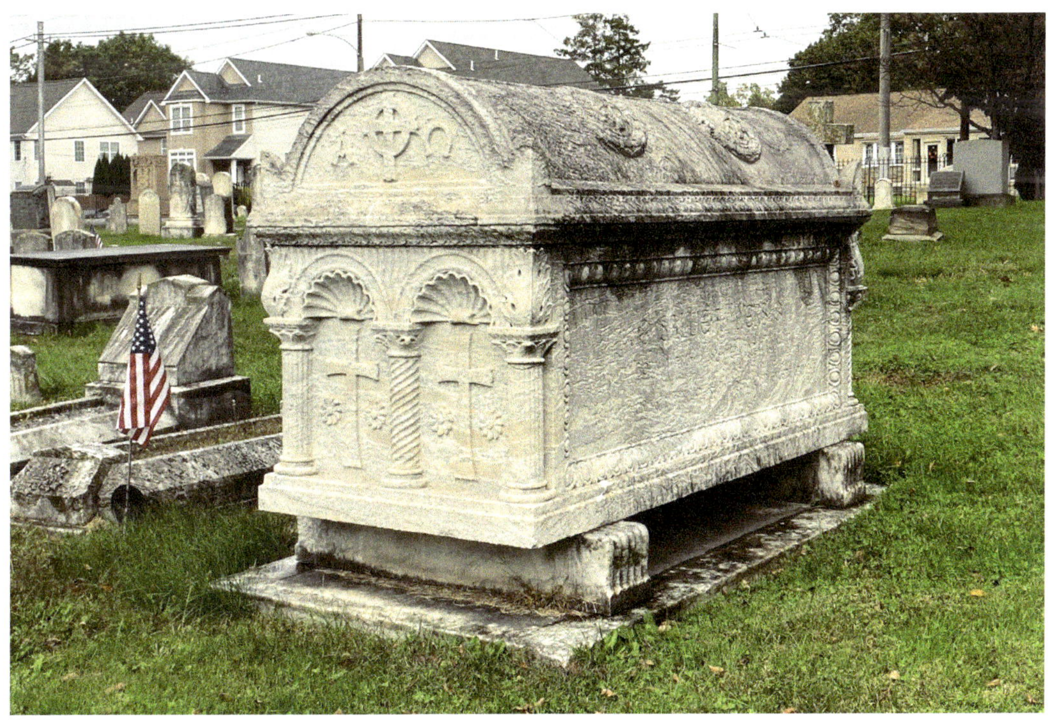

2

# THE RURAL CEMETERY MOVEMENT

The rural cemetery movement in the United States began with Mount Auburn in Cambridge, Massachusetts, in 1831. Philadelphia began to follow suit, and a series of rural cemeteries were founded beginning with the establishment of Laurel Hill East in 1836. Many of these were intentionally situated on the outskirts of the city proper in areas that had previously been part of large farms or estates, and they advertised themselves as being immune from overcrowding or urbanization. As the city boundaries rapidly grew, these once rural locations of course became part of Philadelphia and eventually faced these issues.

Most rural cemeteries were quite large when compared to their predecessors—instead of a few acres sandwiched between buildings, they were 50 to 100 acres or more, often adding parcels incrementally over the years. The grounds were usually highly planned landscapes with attention paid to tree plantings and architectural design; it was not uncommon for a new rural cemetery to hire a well-known architect to design its gatehouse or entryway. It seems each new rural cemetery tried to outdo its neighbors with attempts to attract wealthy clientele who would commission elaborate monuments or mausolea, often hiring the best-known sculptors and artists to produce their statuary and headstones. Some rural cemeteries even had famous Philadelphians disinterred from their original resting place and reburied on their grounds as a means of showcasing the importance of their business.

In addition to being a place of burial, the rural cemeteries were intended to attract visitors to their park-like settings. These cemeteries were often adept marketers, boasting of their prestige in local newspapers and actively working to be considered by citizens as a place to see and be seen. It was not uncommon during this period for people to treat the rural cemeteries as a place of recreation; they might walk the grounds to admire the statues and architecture, have a picnic, spend time sprucing up their families plot, or simply find a shady spot to get respite from the summer heat. Many families have photos of their ancestors enjoying a visit to one of Philadelphia's rural cemeteries, posing not only with their family's headstones but with the grave attractions of people unknown to them.

Despite their grandeur, many of Philadelphia's rural cemeteries have experienced periods of decline and struggle just like their smaller predecessors. In the latter half of the twentieth century, these large properties often fell out of fashion or found that their local communities were less interested in purchasing lots intended for multiple generations of one family. Cremation or other more economical burial options became more attractive, as did burial outside of the city. These conditions, along with fluctuations in Philadelphia's neighborhoods, created strain. Changing attitudes about death and dying also affected the rural cemeteries, although this was certainly not exclusive to one type of burial ground. What was once seen as a place of recreation, relaxation, or reflection came to be viewed as a place one only visited for a funeral or to revisit on an important anniversary. Families became more transient, and people were less likely to live their entire lives in one area so visits to the family's preferred cemetery became less and less frequent.

In a worst-case scenario, Mount Moriah Cemetery (which lies partially in Southwest Philadelphia and partially in Yeadon, Delaware County, Pennsylvania) was abandoned by its owners in 2011. After decades of decline and mounting pressure from families alarmed at the state of the property—which included reports of piles of dumped construction debris, burned out cars, feral dogs, severely overgrown grounds, and lack of monument care—the gate was simply locked and no one returned to work the next day. It's unclear who was managing the operations of the cemetery since its last known living owner died in 2004. In a unique situation, Mount Moriah Cemetery is currently under the care of a receivership and volunteers do all the work to restore and maintain the grounds.

Even in the face of setbacks, most of Philadelphia's rural cemeteries are experiencing a period of vibrant revitalization. They have very few or sometimes no lot sales, and some have reached the point of having no more room for interments other than previously purchased graves. The lack of revenue from lot sales and burials means they have had to imagine new ways of generating funds to provide safekeeping for the grounds. While some may have a sizable endowment that will provide for the necessary care, even those cemeteries have looked to establish revenue streams beyond ordinary operations.

The modern rural cemeteries of Philadelphia are accredited arboreta and have found new ways to bring visitors in through their gates. Places like the Woodlands, Laurel Hill East, and Mount Moriah have moved away from simply being burial grounds, and have established gardening initiatives, vibrant tour programs, and myriad events from concerts and markets to movie nights and birdwatching. While the cemeteries continue to exist as sacred spaces, they have also sought to reinvent themselves and reestablish the rural cemetery as a place to visit for recreation and relaxation like people did during the Victorian era. This certainly has not changed everyone's mind of course, but all these locations have seen steady increases to the number of visitors each year in recent times.

Because of the intentional grandeur of the rural cemeteries, these are often the best places for cemetery sightseeing. One could spend hours walking the grounds and still feel like there is more to encounter. In fact, in this photographer's experience, each visit to any of Philadelphia's rural cemeteries seems very familiar, but also like visiting for the first time. Around the bend in each pathway or beyond a hill, there is likely a monument never noticed before with a story waiting to be told or seasonal changes to the landscape that draw the eye to something new.

It is also worth noting that the size of the rural cemeteries brings to light the fact that thousands of burials are not marked in any way. When visiting most cemeteries, there will be obvious gaps between headstones in neatly aligned rows or simply open areas with less of a concentration of markers. It is a common misconception that all burials have some sort of gravestone, and family history researchers sometimes assume the marker existed but has been buried or damaged. Grave markers have always been expensive, and many families simply could not afford them, especially when considering the higher mortality rates of the time. As you walk the grounds, there will be many open areas with no gravestone or monument, but chances are high that burials are everywhere under foot.

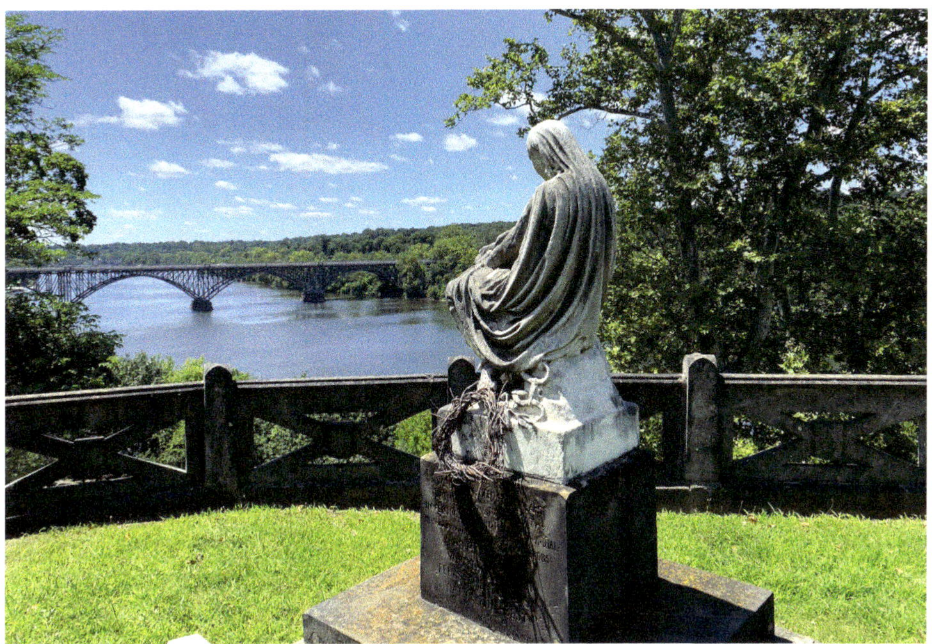

Laurel Hill East was established in 1836, the second cemetery in the new "rural cemetery" movement that began with Mount Auburn (Massachusetts) in a bid to move burial grounds out of the city center and away from urbanization. Laurel Hill is situated in the East Falls neighborhood and overlooks the Schuylkill River.

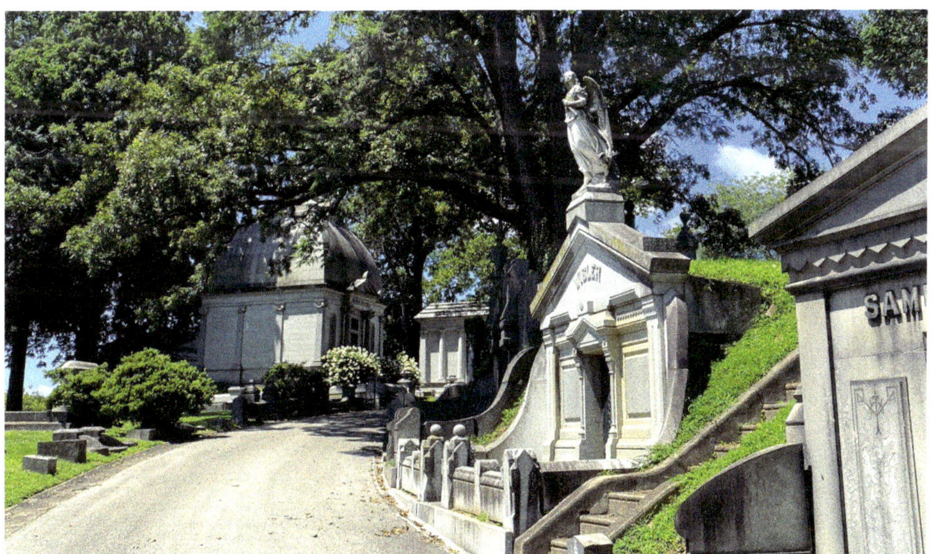

Many of the city's elite, white Protestants built extravagant mausolea, crypts, and statuary to honor their dead and outdo the neighbors. Families commissioned well-known artists and architects to design monuments, and the cemetery quickly became a tourist destination for people interested in exploring the artwork and landscape.

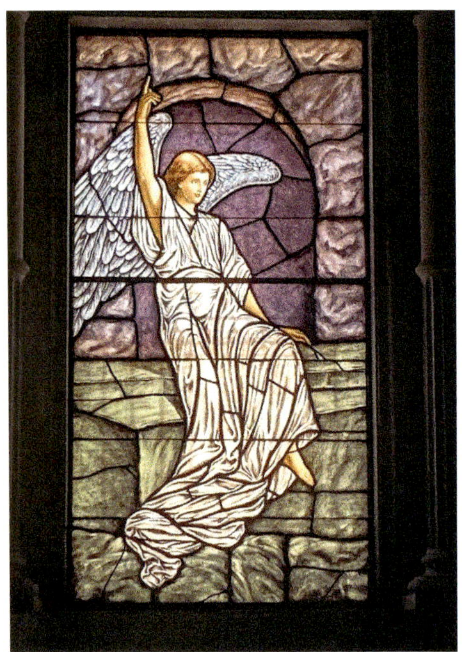

*Left:* With such a large number of mausolea in one place, it's no surprise that many of them have exquisite stained-glass windows at the back which can be seen through the doorway. Laurel Hill East has a number of such windows manufactured by Tiffany Glass.

*Below:* From 1870 through World War I, "white bronze" memorials—made of zinc and copper alloys—became popular because they could be mass produced and ordered via catalog from Connecticut's Monumental Bronze Company. Made of separate panels, these monuments have stood the test of time better than many of their stone counterparts, with only the seams where the panels were bolted or fused experiencing deterioration.

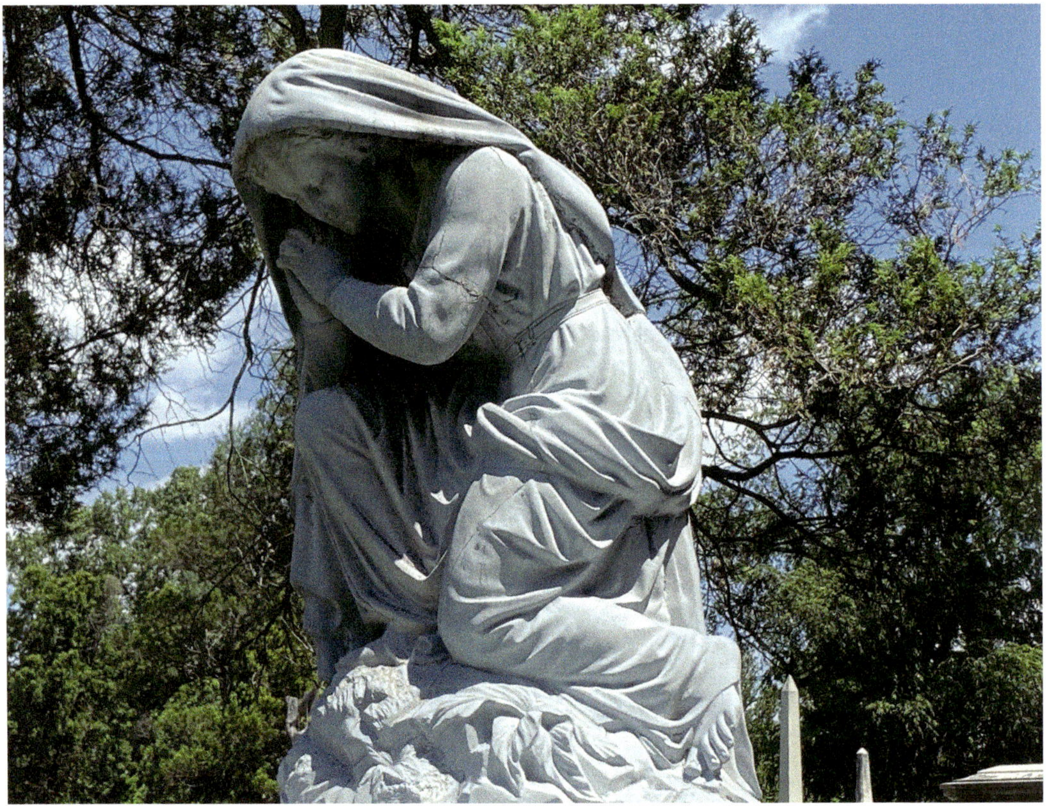

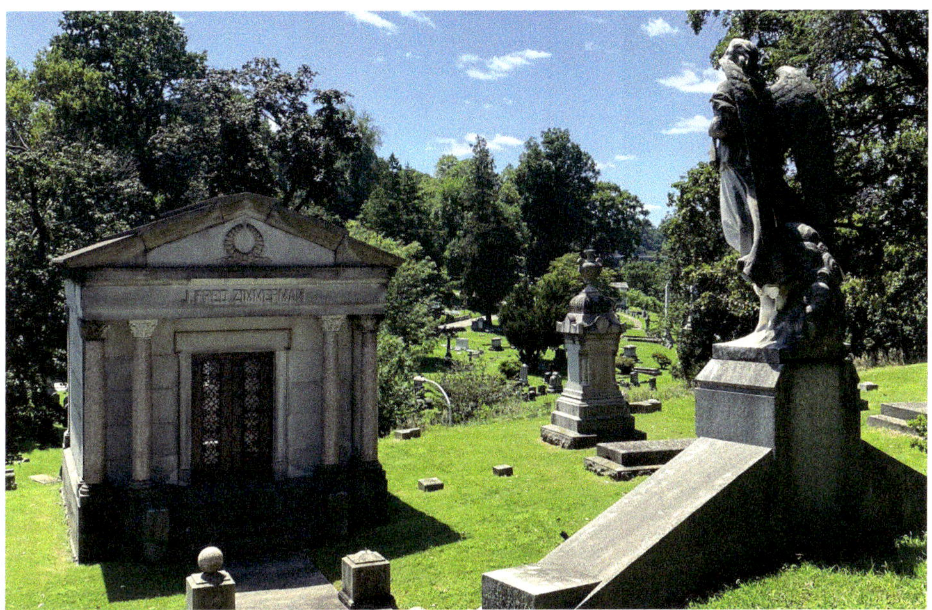

Laurel Hill East is an exquisitely landscaped arboretum that offered visitors a park-like experience in the days before public parks were established in Philadelphia.

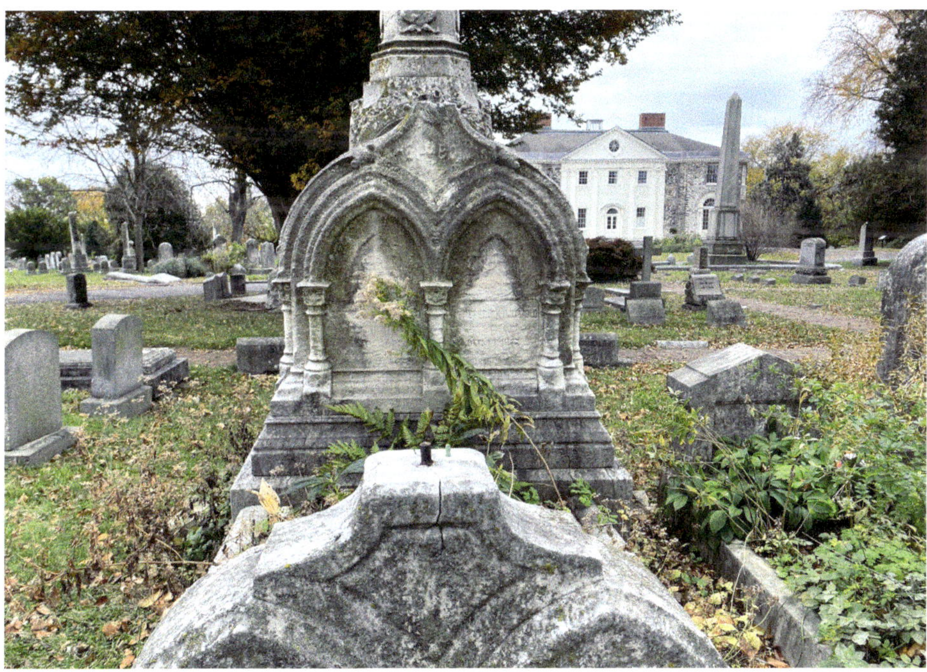

The Woodlands is situated on the former Hamilton estate, which botanist William Hamilton planted with many plant species before the cemetery was established in 1840. The mansion seen in the background of this photograph is used today for special events and cemetery staff offices.

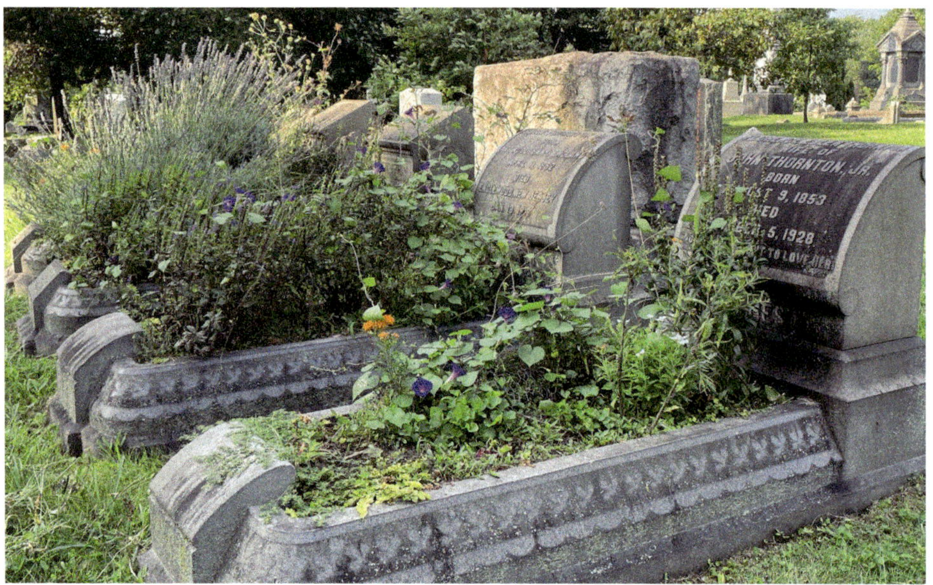

The cemetery features a large number of Victorian-era "cradle graves," named because of their bed-like style of a headstone, footstone, and low walls with the space in between meant for plantings. The Woodlands has a very active Grave Gardeners program where volunteers plant and care for one or more cradle graves throughout the growing season.

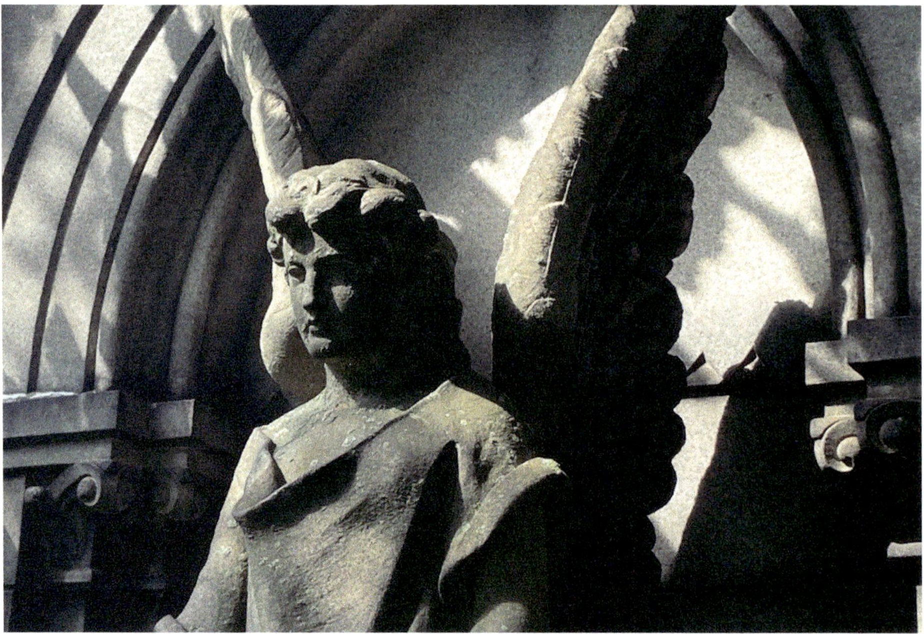

Although not as flashy as Laurel Hill East, the Woodlands still contains a wide variety of ornate monuments and statuary, including the large archway featuring two angels and the epitaph, "Through Darkness to the Light."

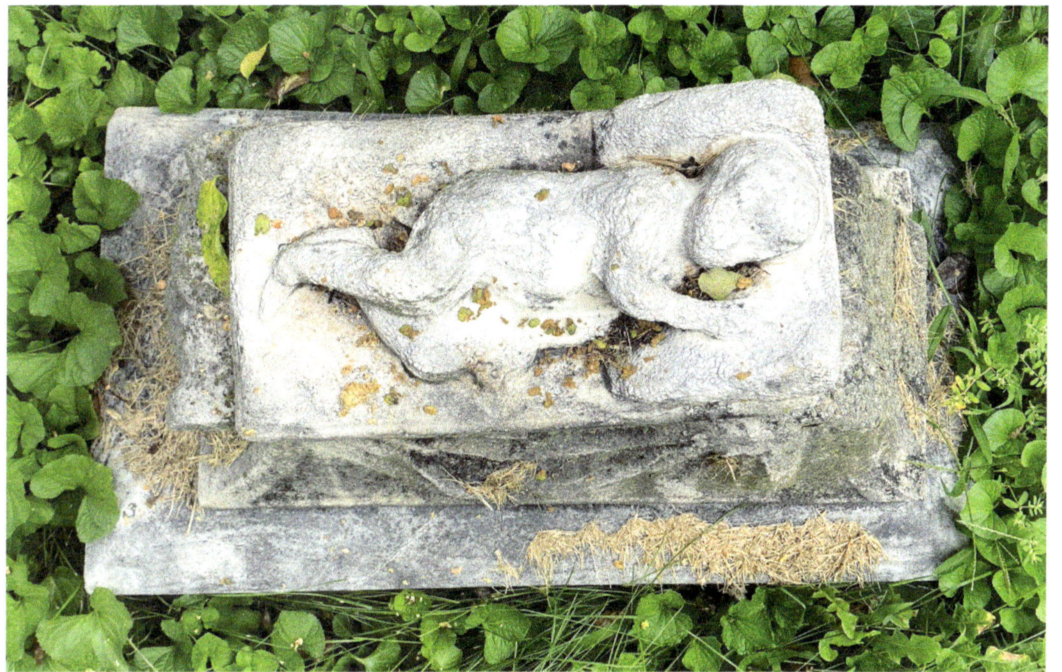

The Woodlands certainly includes the graves of many Philadelphians who were not considered wealthy or elite but were no less important to their families. This carving of a young child sleeping is a beautiful, but stark reminder of the number of babies that did not reach adulthood.

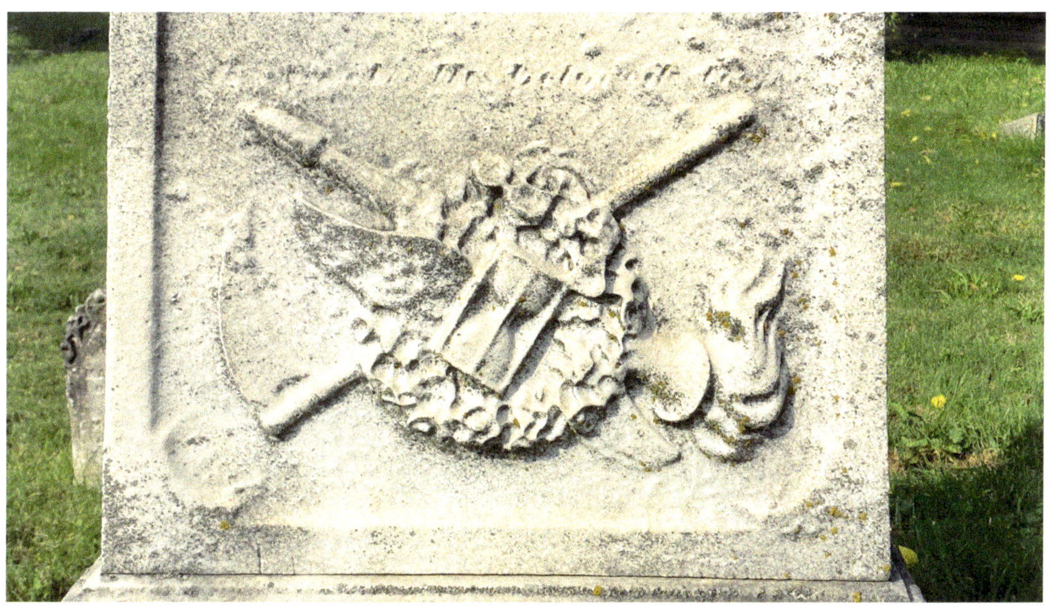

The winged hourglass is the graphic representation of *Tempus fugit*, or "time flies."

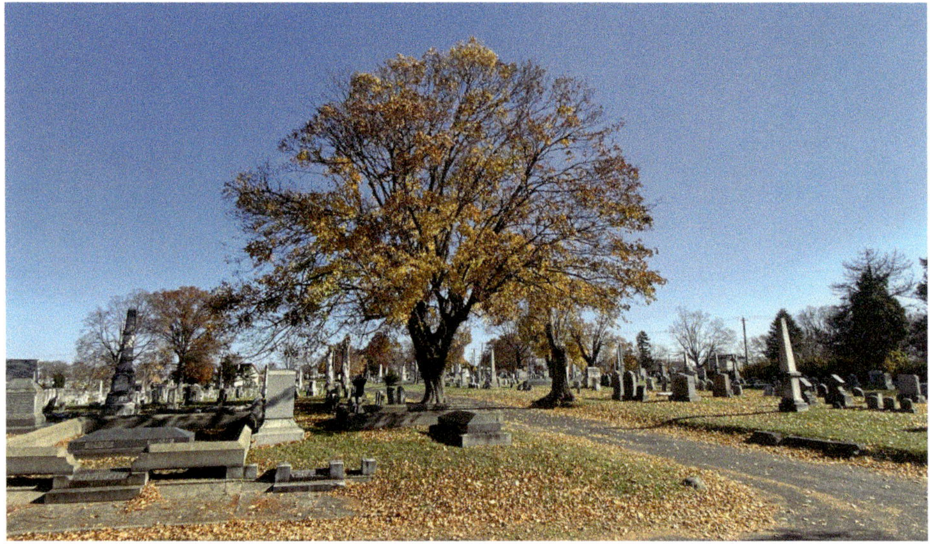

Cedar Hill Cemetery would be considered part of the rural cemetery movement due to its founding in 1850 and its size, although it seems to have fallen on hard times. It's clear that the property with winding roads and mature trees was once very well cared for and maintained.

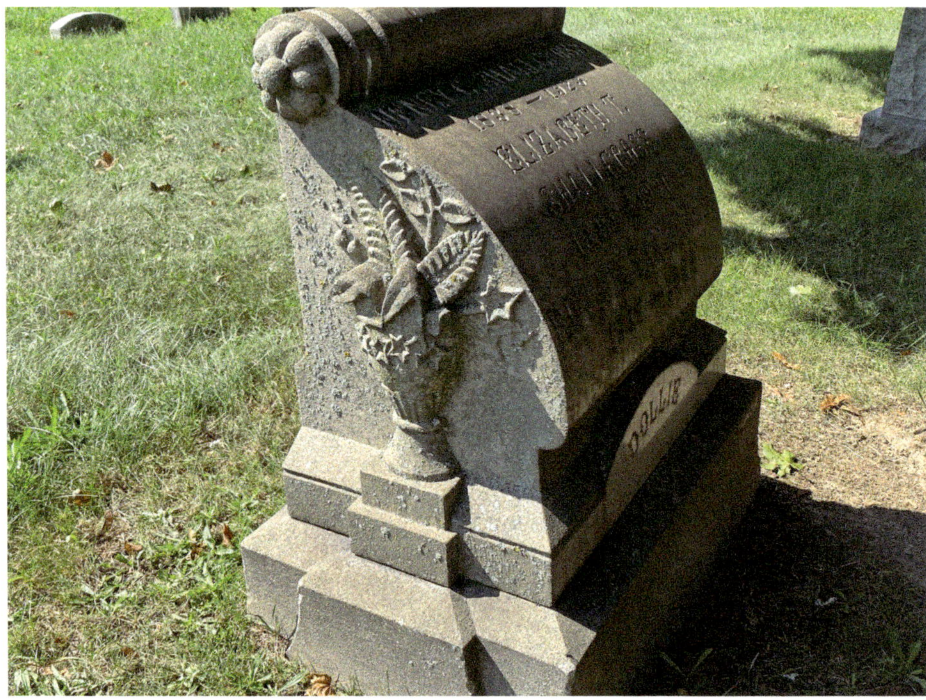

There are some beautiful carving specimens, like the vase and bouquet on the side of the Shallcross family marker.

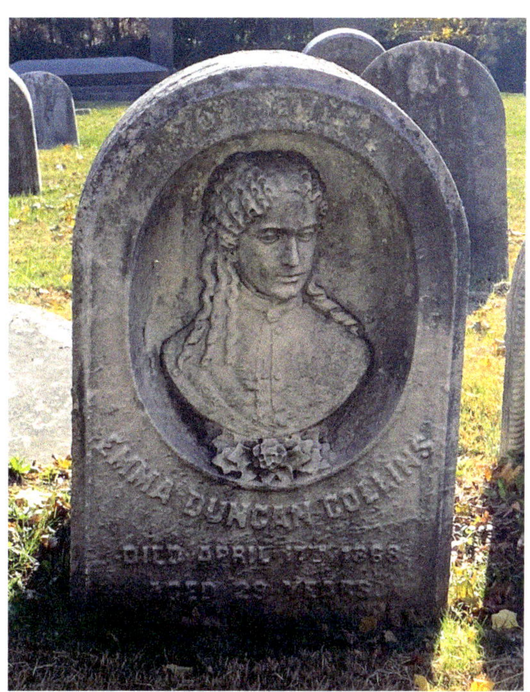

*Right:* The gravestone for Emma Duncan Collins, who died in 1898, has a gorgeous carving of her likeness with exceptional detail on her hair and face that has survived well over 120 years with no damage.

*Below:* Cedar Hill shows a number of signs of vandalism and even rituals involving what appears to be chicken bones and feathers carried out atop some gravestones. This once-beautiful monument had a statue in pieces and evidence of these types of religious practices.

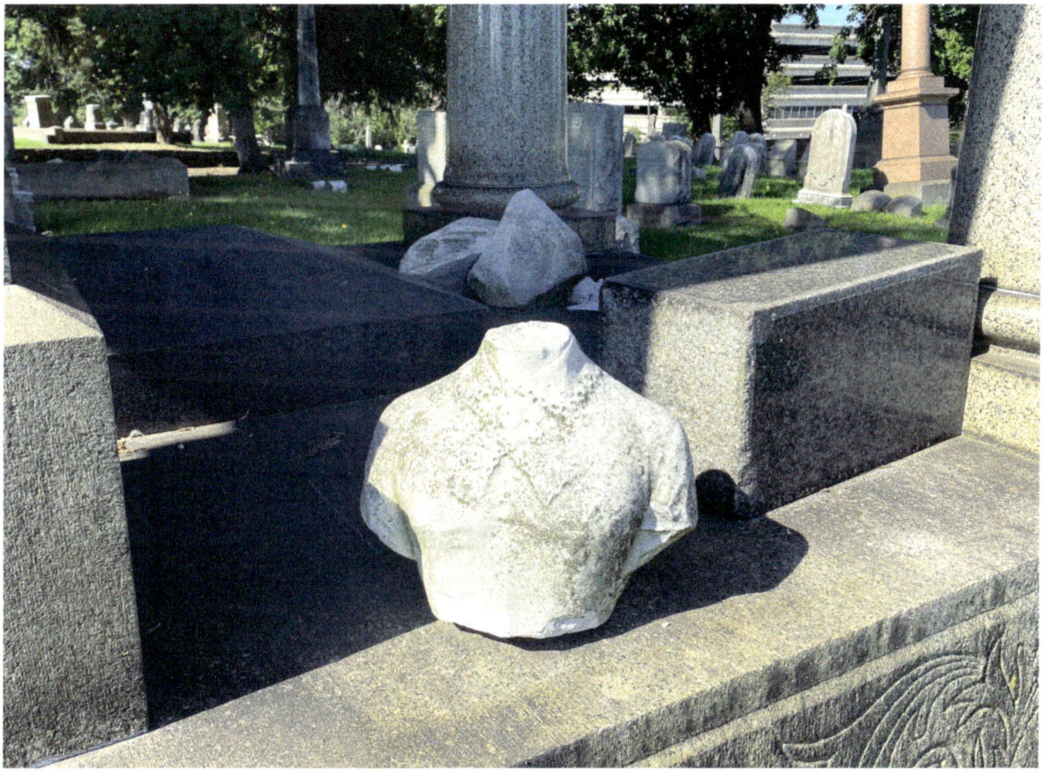

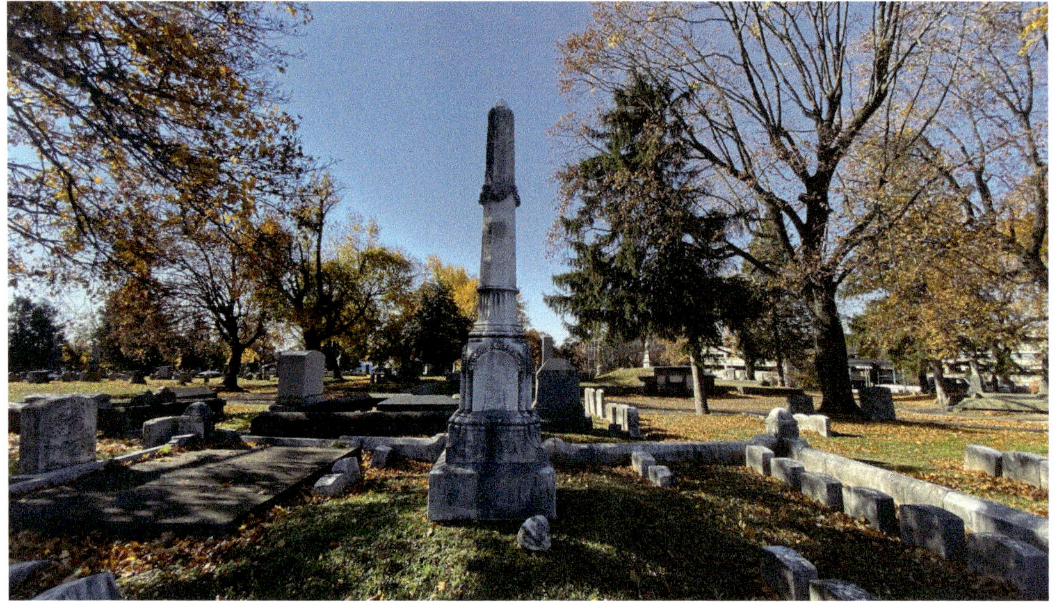

The cemetery still seems to be active, although it's not clear to what extent or what entity manages the property.

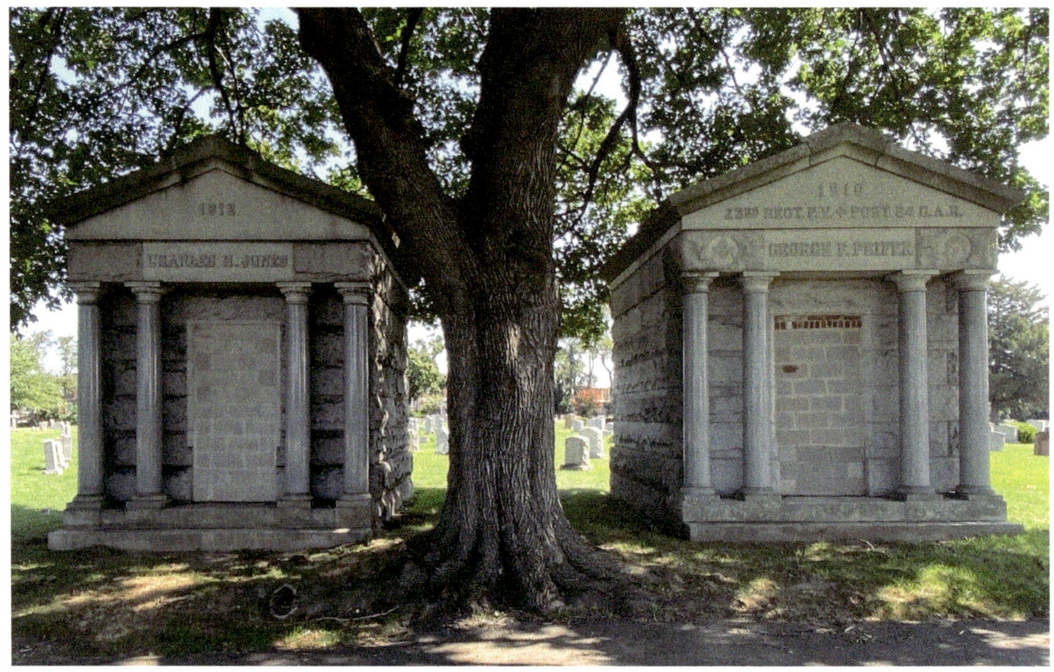

It's not obvious whether North Cedar Hill, across the street from Cedar Hill, is directly related or whether these were always distinct properties. The grounds are fairly indistinct, and it appears the property has been struggling, as displayed by this pair of mausolea closed up with cinder blocks.

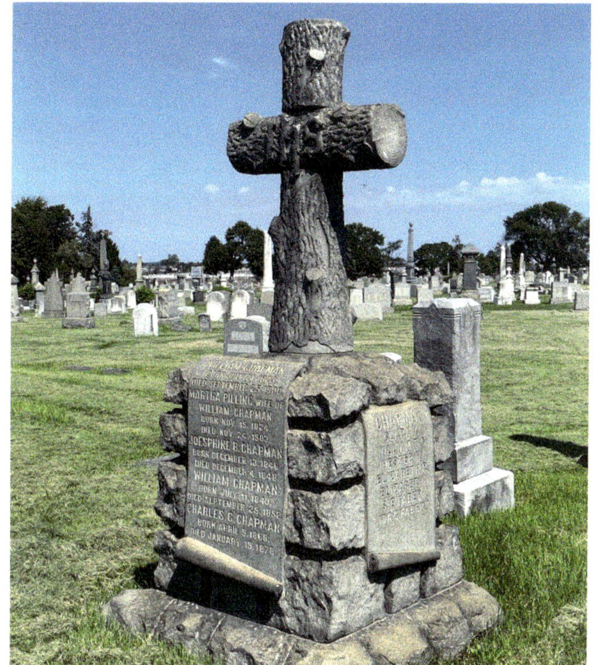

The cemetery does have some gorgeous examples of nineteenth and twentieth century gravestones, including this cross-shaped tree stump tombstone with scroll work on the base.

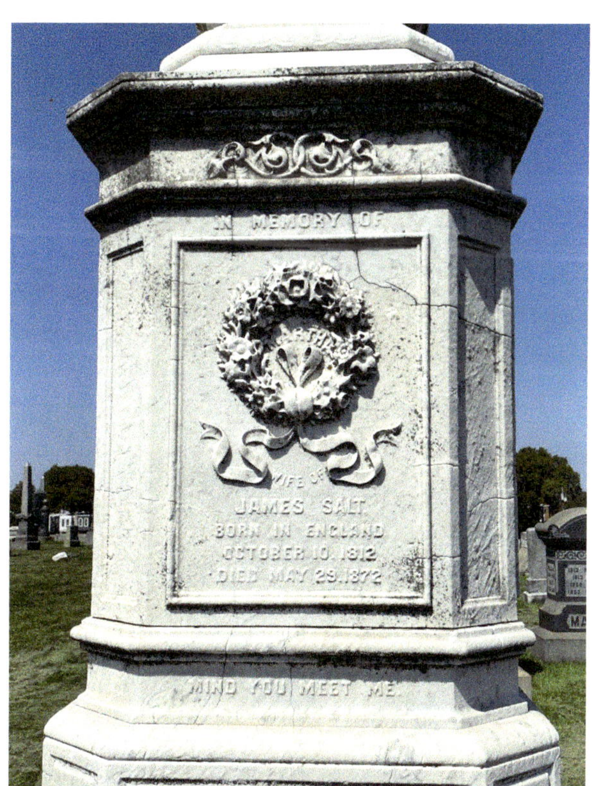

Martha Salt's monument includes an intricately carved wreath bearing her first name and the epitaph, "Mind you meet me."

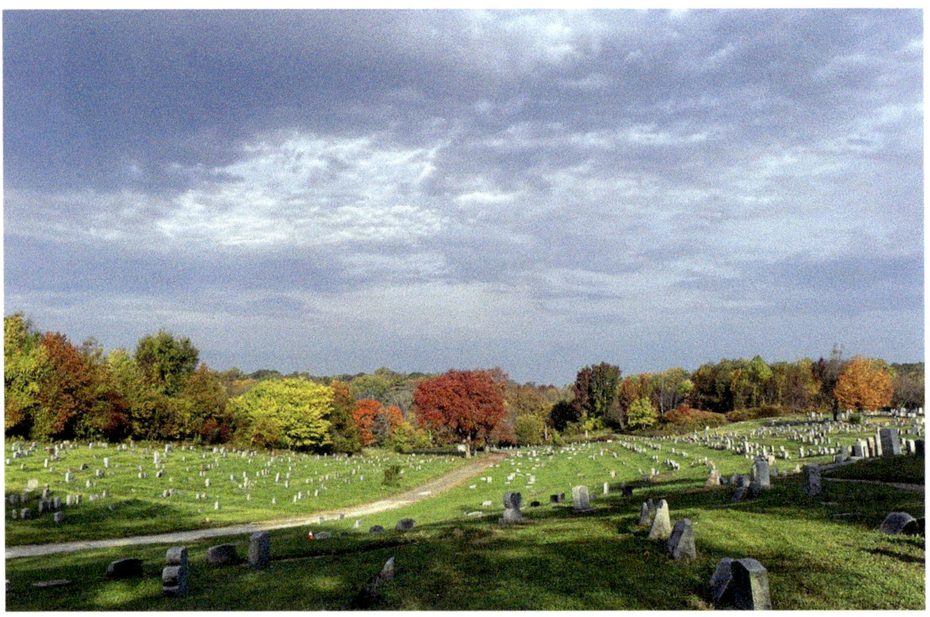

Mount Moriah Cemetery was established in 1855 and abandoned by its owners in 2011. Since then, a dedicated group of volunteers has been working to restore the nearly 200-acre property which bisects Philadelphia and Delaware Counties.

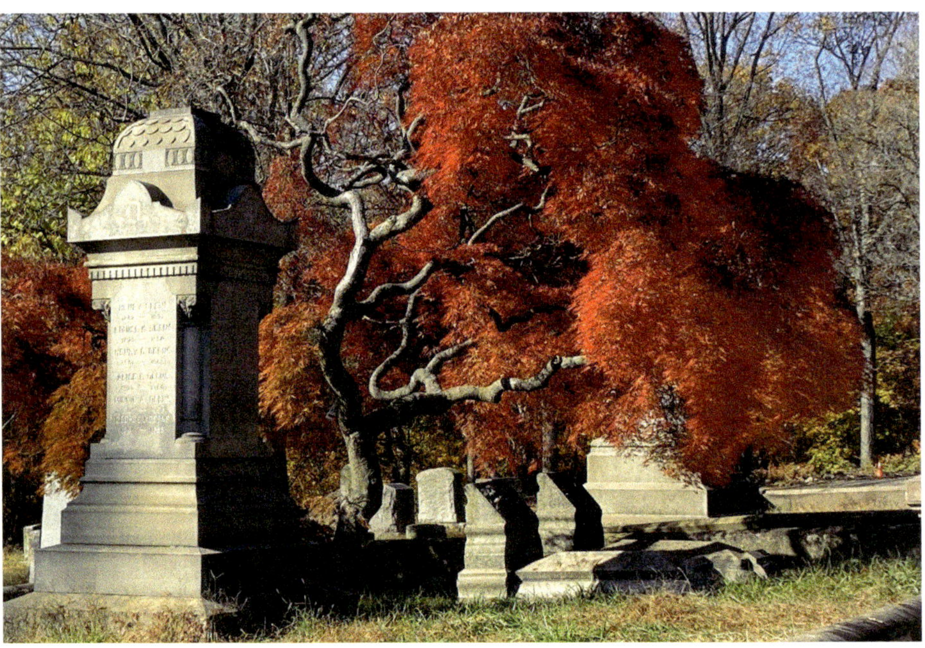

This cemetery, like many others from the rural cemetery movement, is an arboretum featuring many species of trees. The Japanese maple at the Deens-Maull plot is particularly striking year-round.

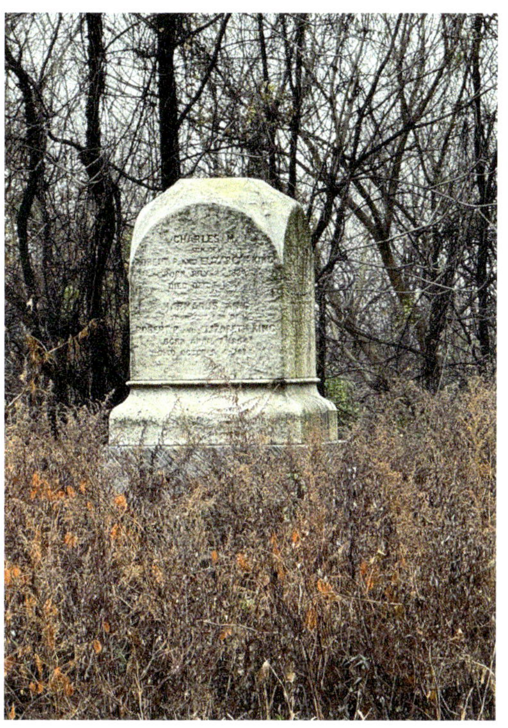

*Right:* The volunteer group has cleared about 70% of the cemetery grounds since 2011, but there are many areas that are still overgrown and inaccessible to visitors.

*Below:* Since Mount Moriah didn't cater to an exclusively wealthy clientele, there are less grand mausolea and statues there, although this statue atop the Galbraith family plot is a fine example of the craftsmanship you can easily find while taking a stroll through the grounds.

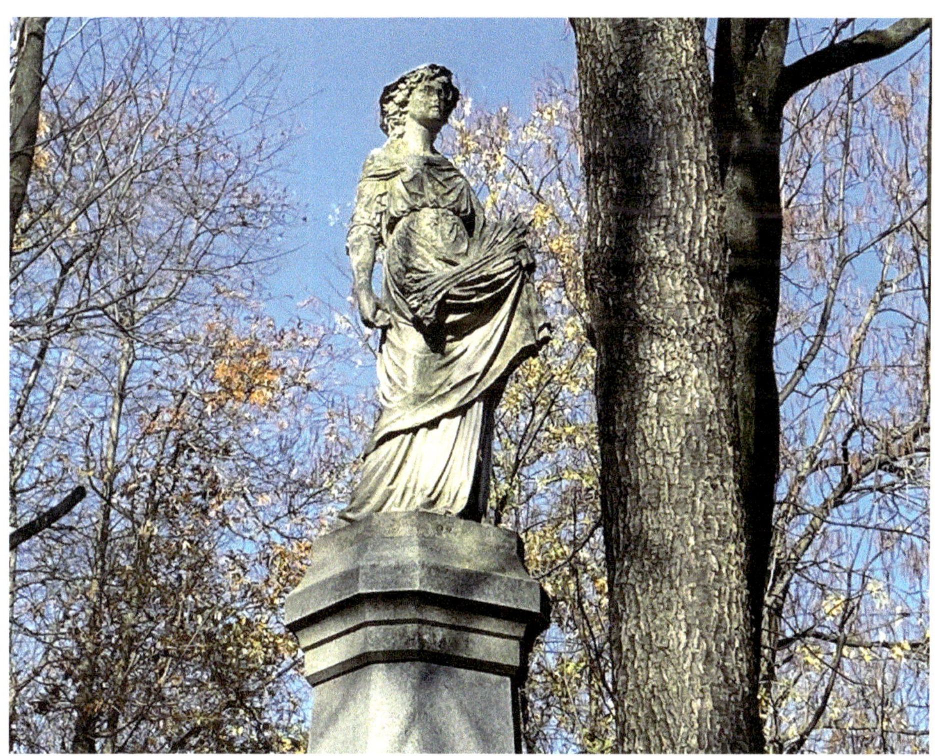

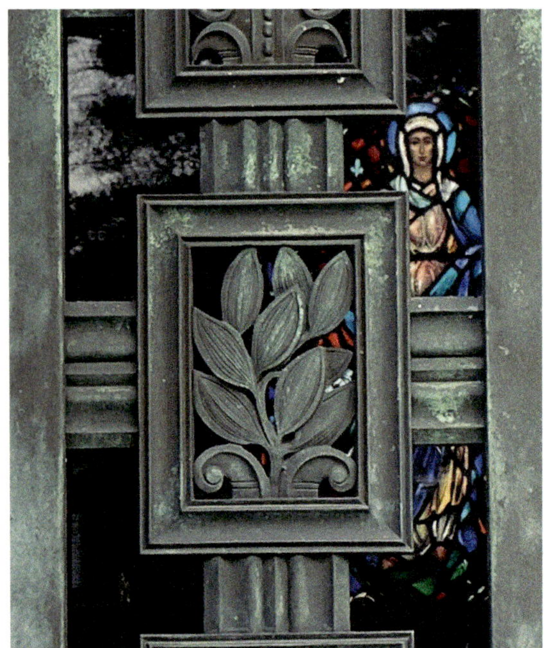

*Left:* Of the small number of mausoleums, only a few still have their original doors and stained glass.

*Below:* Many of the gravestones and monuments have fallen victim to time, gravity, or vandalism, especially during the decades the cemetery was not being well taken care of as lot sales declined.

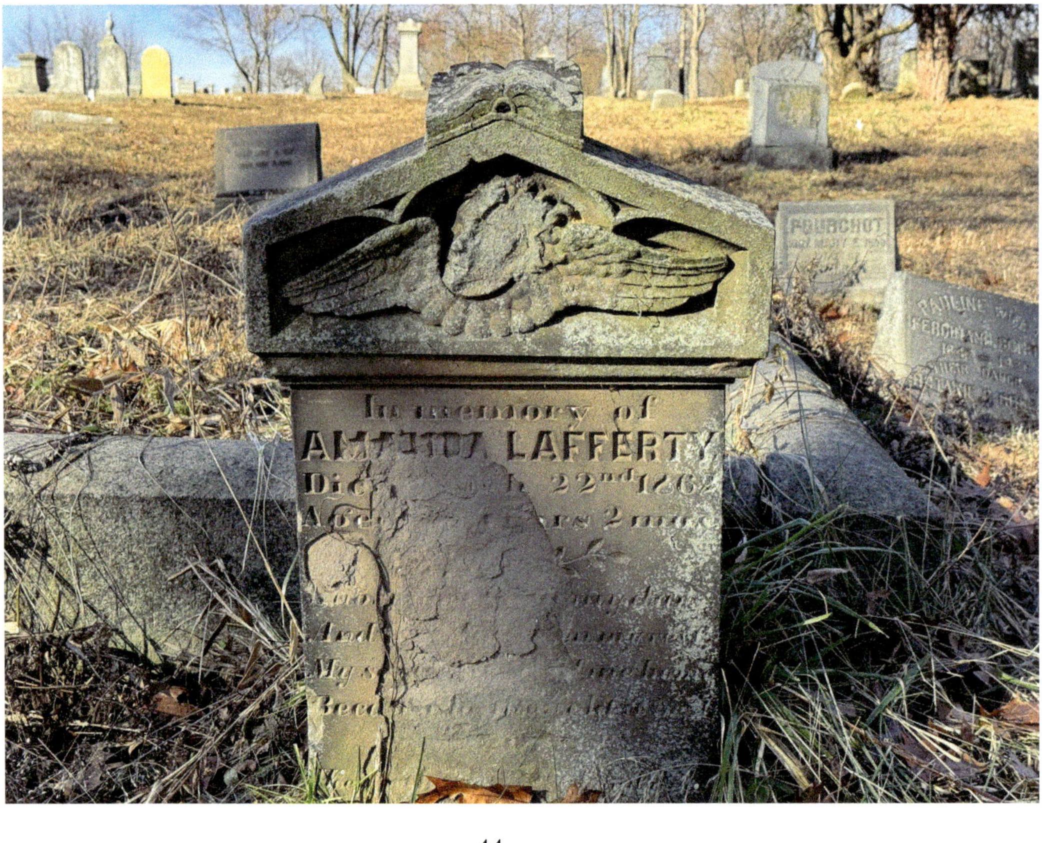

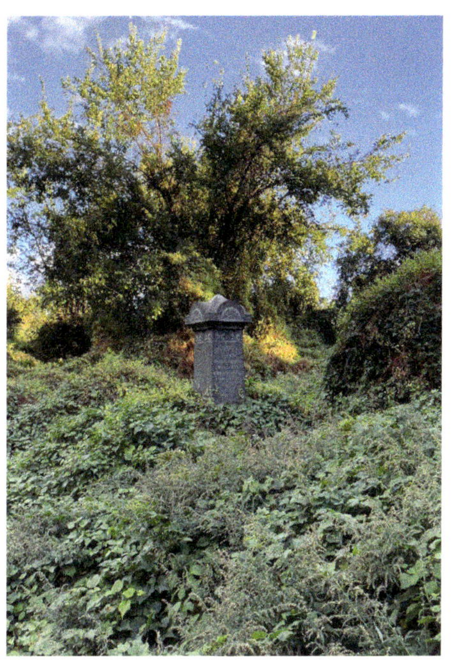

*Right:* Mount Vernon Cemetery, the last of Philadelphia's rural cemetery movement, was established in 1856. Since the 1970s, the owner of the property did not sell new lots, and the cemetery fell into disrepair. It was placed under a conservatorship in 2021 and a large portion of the 27-acre property remains quite overgrown.

*Below:* Mount Vernon's most recognizable monument is the pyramid-shaped memorial for Julia Gardel, depicted in relief above the door. It was erected by her husband, who would later be interred with his wife in the vault below. The statues depict America and some of the places Julia, an avid traveler who died in Syria, had visited.

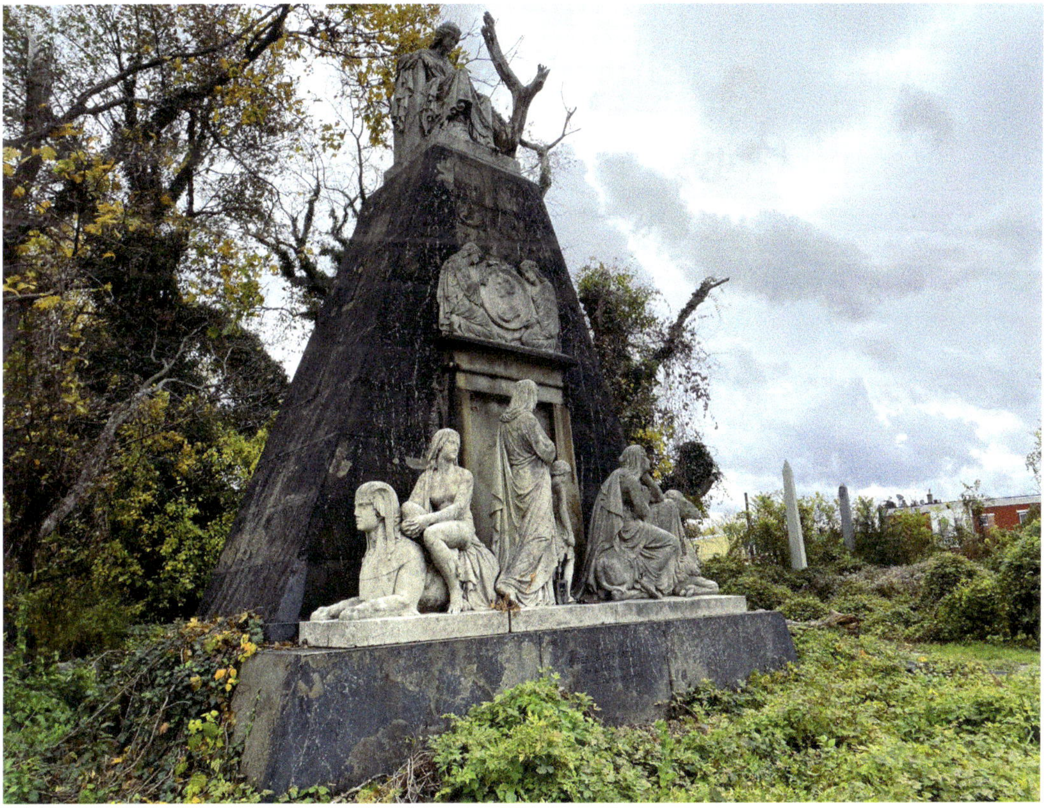

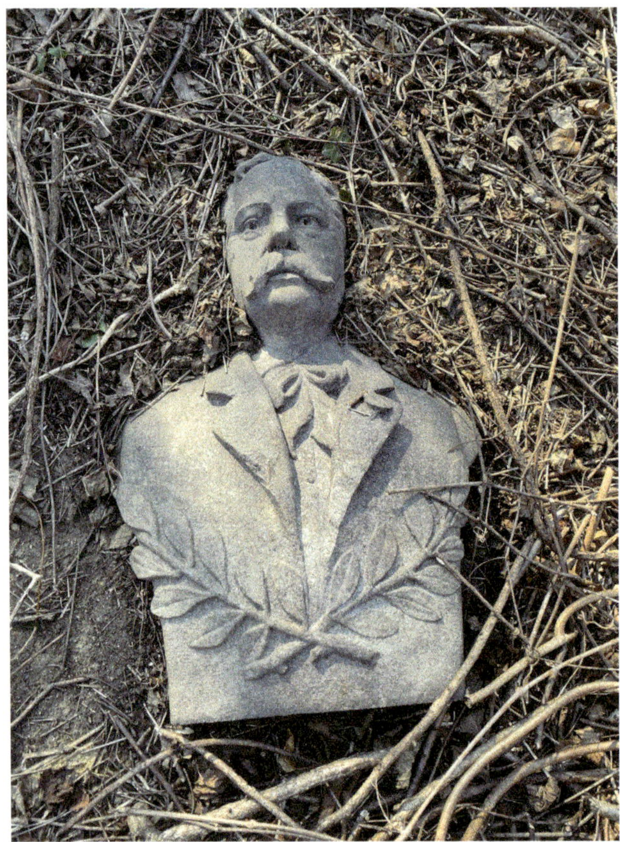

*Left:* From visits over the past few years, it's clear there's a lot of exciting gravestones just waiting to be fully uncovered.

*Below:* Mt. Sinai is one of the oldest Jewish cemeteries in the city, established in 1854. As part of the rural cemetery movement, the grounds are well landscaped with mature trees, winding paths, large mausolea and monuments, and a chapel designed by renowned architect Frank Furness.

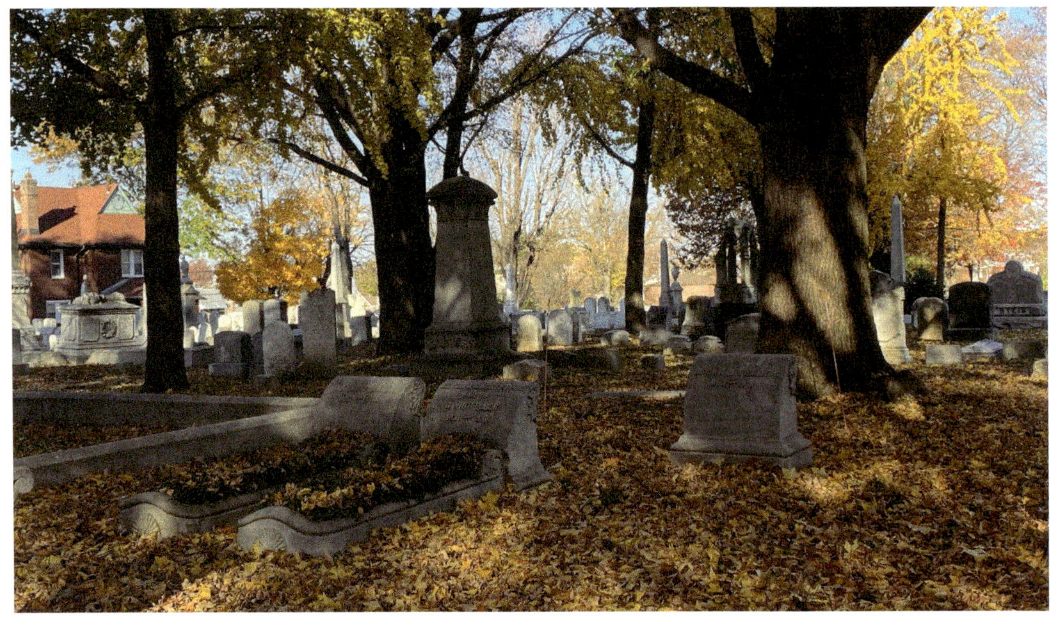

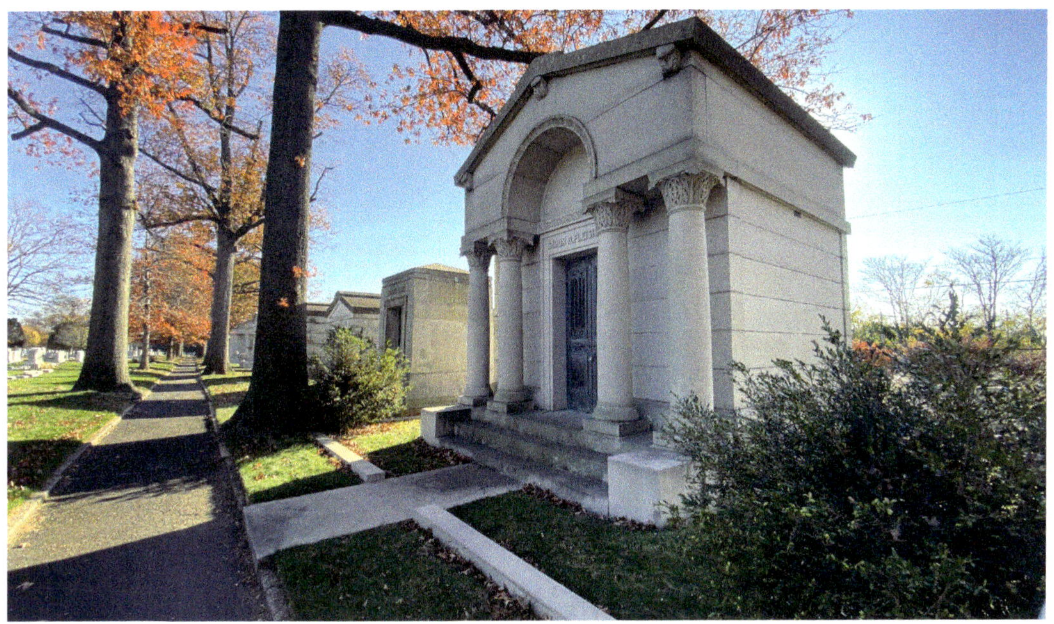

*Above:* Just inside Mt. Sinai's entry gate is a long row of stately mausolea that are just a few examples of memorials to many of Philadelphia's early, prominent Jewish families.

*Right:* While some mausolea have seen better days—including one with a misspelling forever etched in stone above the door—there are some gorgeous examples of stained-glass masterpieces visible to anyone curious enough to peer inside.

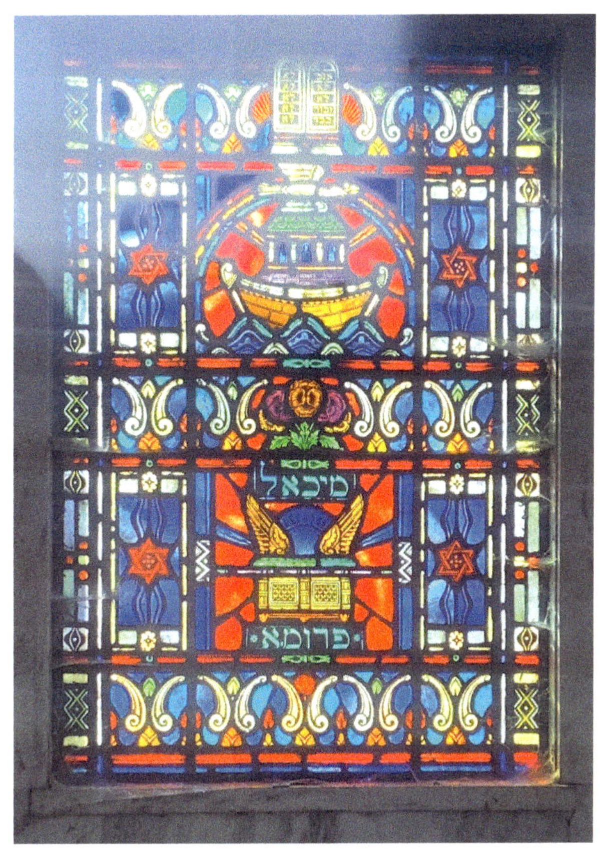

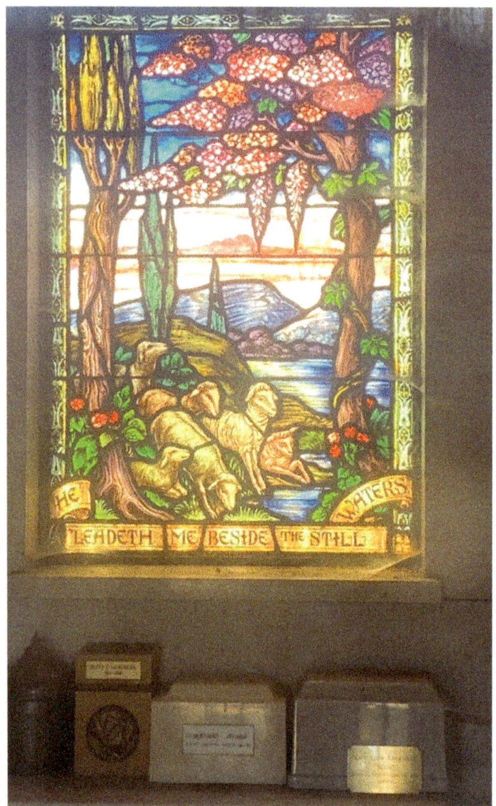

*Left:* In addition to intricately colored and patterned stained glass, it's not uncommon to see cremation urns on the interior ledges of an otherwise full mausoleum.

*Below:* Even the oldest gravestones have exceptional detail to the carvings, showcasing the care families gave to their deceased loved ones.

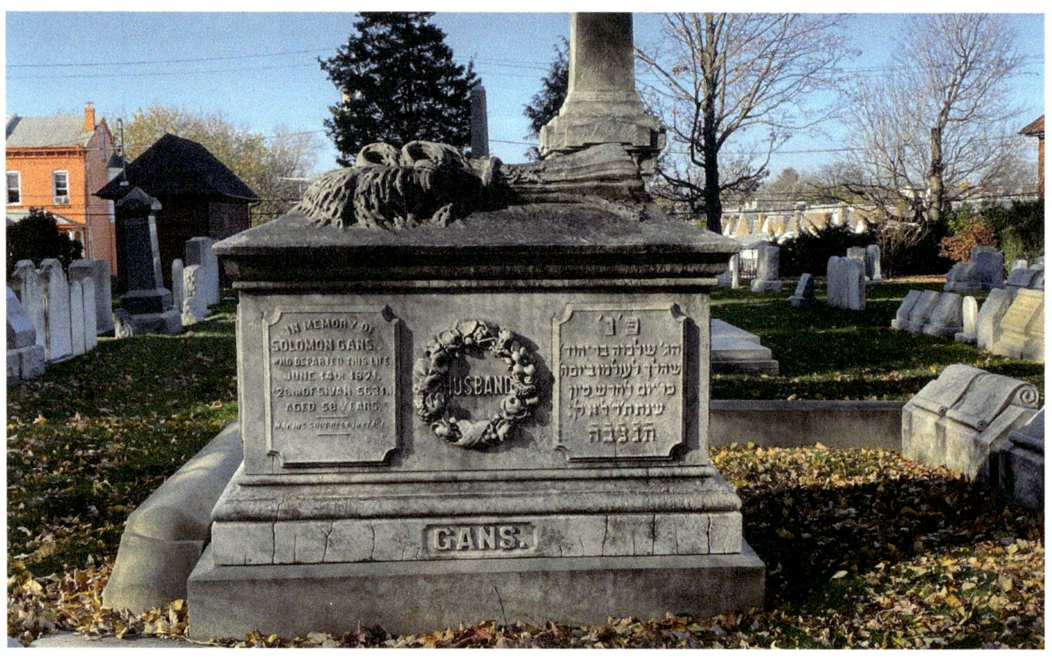

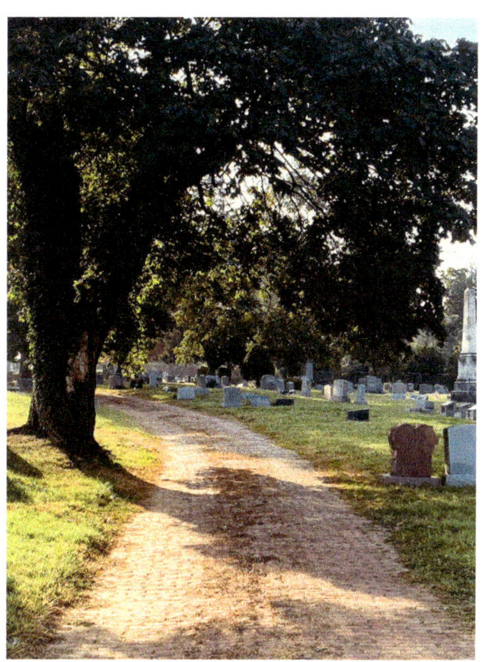

*Right:* Mount Peace Cemetery, adjacent to Mount Vernon and across the street from Laurel Hill East, was established on part of a former estate by the same name.

*Below:* This Odd Fellows cemetery includes some grand monuments to members of the fraternal order, such as this detailed gravestone for William Curtis (1812-1868), which features his likeness in relief on one side.

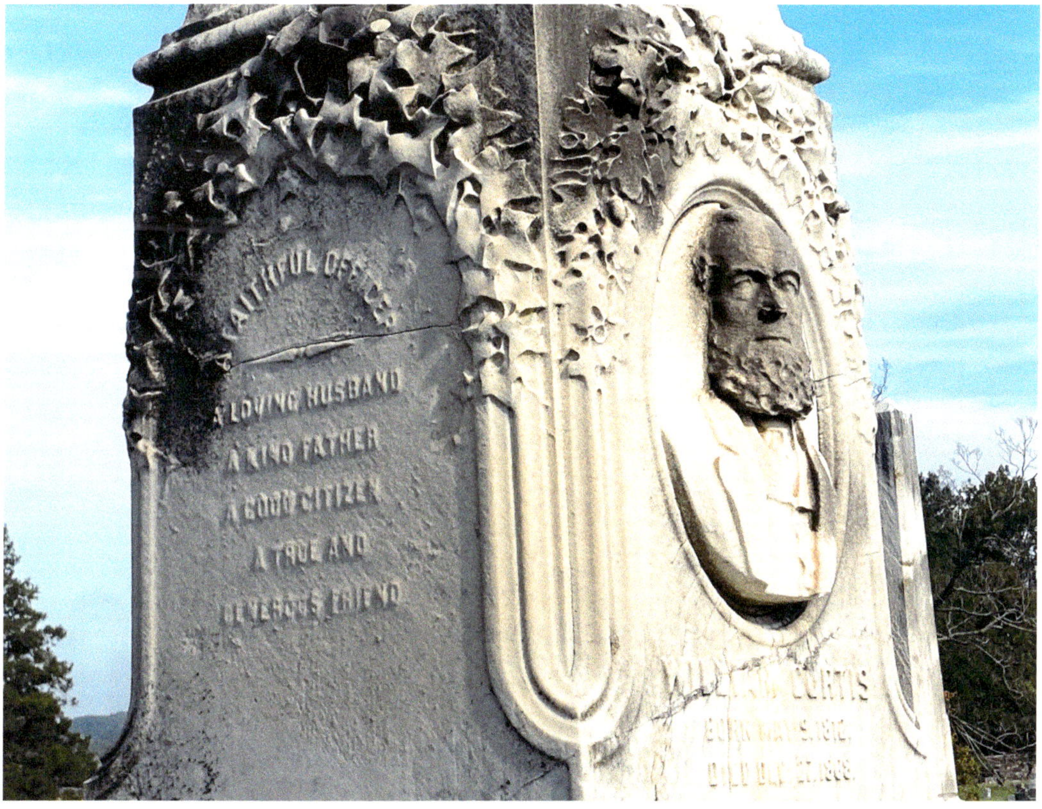

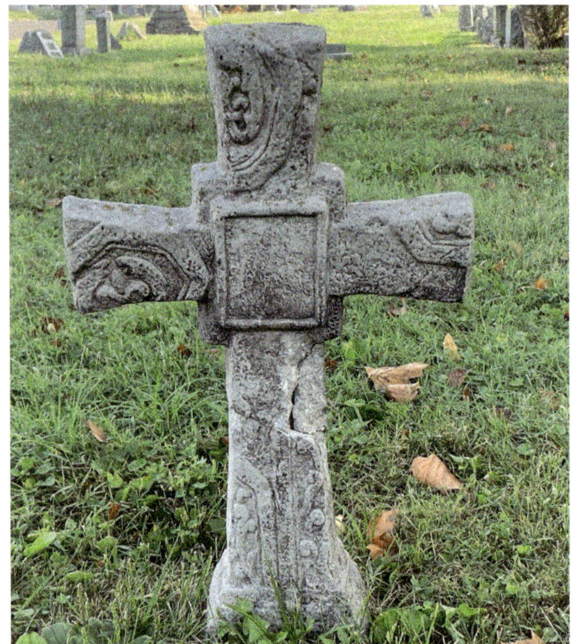

*Left:* Many people find it surprising how many graves in most cemeteries are unmarked. What is perhaps more of an eye-opener are the number of graves that have a marker that don't appear to have ever had an inscription identifying the interment.

*Below:* Changing with the times, it appears Mount Peace has established a cremation interment or scatter area that was filled with dozens of standard funeral home markers.

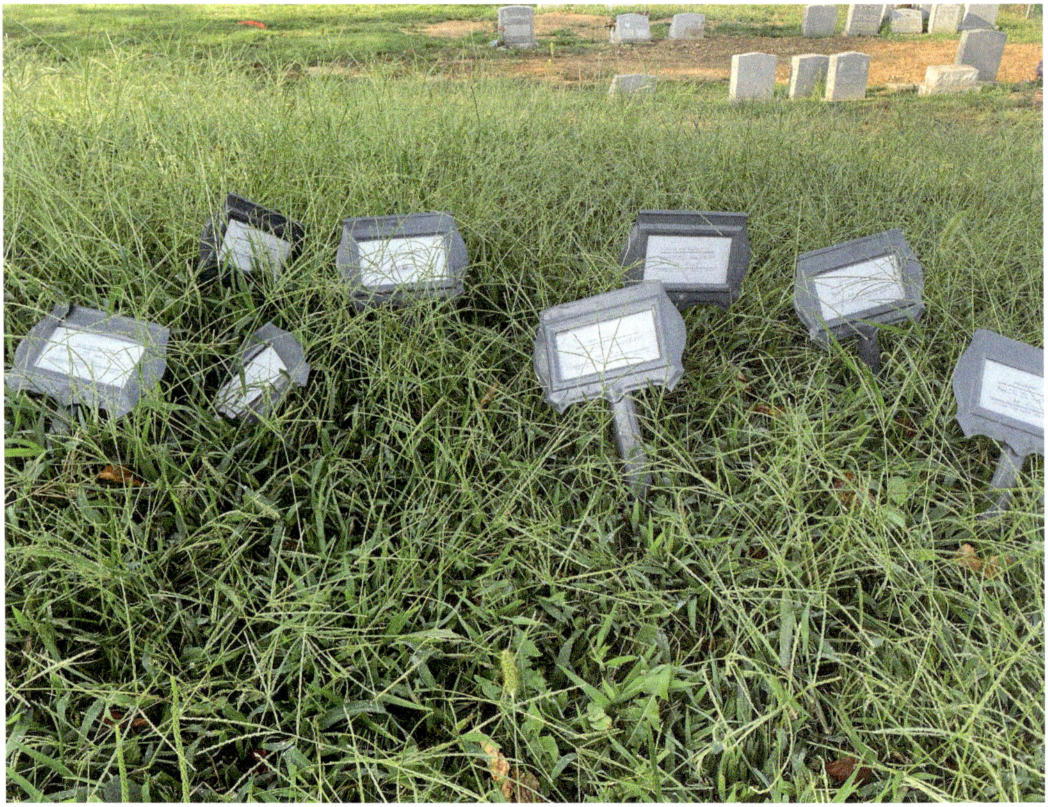

<h1 style="text-align:center">3<br>NEW GROUND FOR AN EXPANDING POPULATION</h1>

Throughout the first half of the nineteenth century, there were still other burial grounds being established in Philadelphia that were not part of the rural cemetery movement. While some of them predate the Victorian-era trend of carefully landscaped burial grounds intended to be park-like destinations filled with sculpture, the new cemeteries in this period were all founded by religious communities that sought space to accommodate the growing population of the city that was in turn increasing their own membership. If one thinks about the rural cemetery movement as a clear design and marketing choice often established as a money-making venture, the cemeteries that were founded in this group continued the Colonial-era tradition of simply meeting a need to care for the dead. Religious oriented burial grounds are how structured cemetery spaces in Philadelphia began and how they predominantly continued for generations.

Philadelphia was no longer the nation's capital by this point, but that did not slow down the city's expansion. One can easily see where immigrant populations arriving in Philadelphia were making their homes based on where churches and synagogues were being built. Catholic, Presbyterian, Jewish, Lutheran, Episcopal, and other congregations created new houses of worship and established burial sites for their membership. Cathedral Cemetery in West Philadelphia, often called "Old" Cathedral because it predates the New Cathedral Cemetery, is perhaps the largest of this group of eleven locations. It seems Cathedral is still accepting new burials, but many of the cemeteries initiated in this period are no longer active and have not been for many years. Still, an adventurous cemetery tourist would be remiss to not include these burial grounds on a complete tour of Philadelphia's graveyards.

Other cemeteries featured in this chapter sprung up to serve congregants near areas of industry, such as Bethany German Lutheran or St. Timothy's Episcopal and St. David's Episcopal chuchyards in Manayunk. The Manayunk area, and its neighbor up the hill, Roxborough, were hubs of textile production and other types of manufacturing for well over 100 years due to the close proximity to the Schuylkill River and the Manayunk

Canal. Mill workers and the wealthy factory owners needed places close by to worship and also bury their dead, and the new churches accommodated their religious needs. As factories in these areas began to close in the twentieth century, usage of these churches and their graveyards dwindled as membership steadily decreased. Whether the church itself is still operational today or not, the cemetery properties were generally the first to close either because they had filled up or due to the overhead cost of maintaining a graveyard.

The story is similar for Saint James the Less Episcopal Churchyard in the Allegheny West neighborhood. It too had become a home to not only wealthy landowners, but industrial laborers in the nearby factories. Although the graveyard of Saint James the Less does not rise to the size of a rural cemetery, its location was chosen for its pastoral setting. The American Gothic church here is apparently a near replica of an English parish church, and even today, the grounds could not be more beautiful with tree-lined walkways and endless rows of headstones. Although one side of the Saint James the Less property overlooks the very busy West Hunting Park Avenue corridor and the overall setting is quite urban, the churchyard is a quiet refuge from the flurry of activity that surrounds it.  If you live near or are visiting Philadelphia, the grounds of Saint James the Less are well worth a visit in any season; you might feel transported to the English countryside.

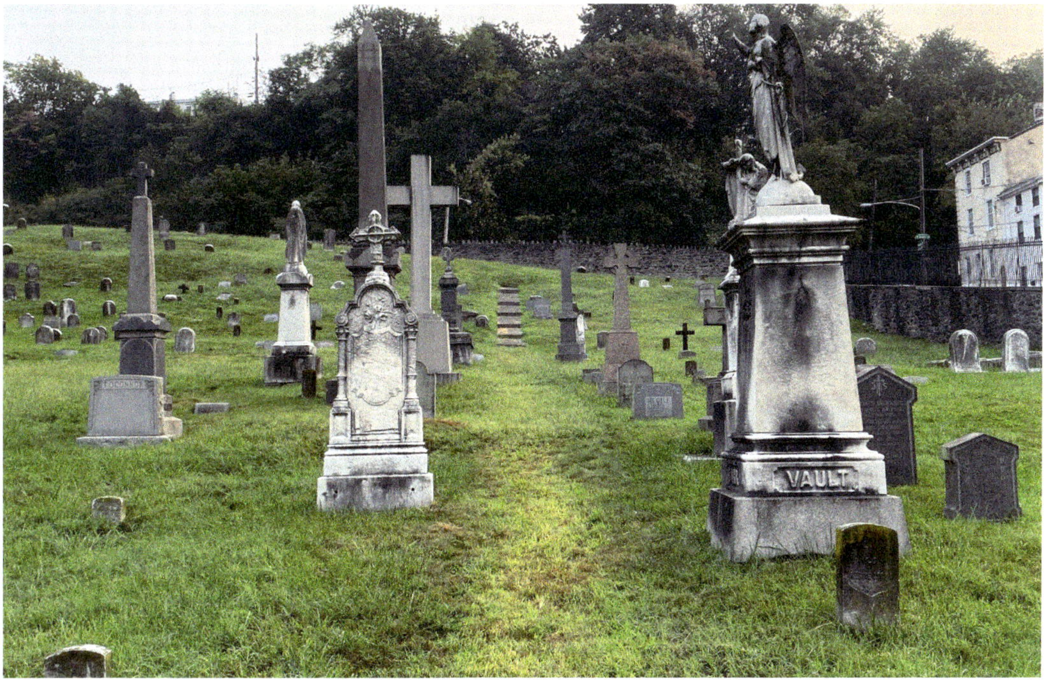

*Above:* St. John the Baptist Catholic Church Cemetery, in the Manayunk neighborhood of Philadelphia, was established around 1830, with the burial grounds laid out on a steep hillside that is common in this area.

*Right:* Manayunk began as a mill town, and the evidence of industry surrounds the property with the elevated train tracks visible just across Cresson Street.

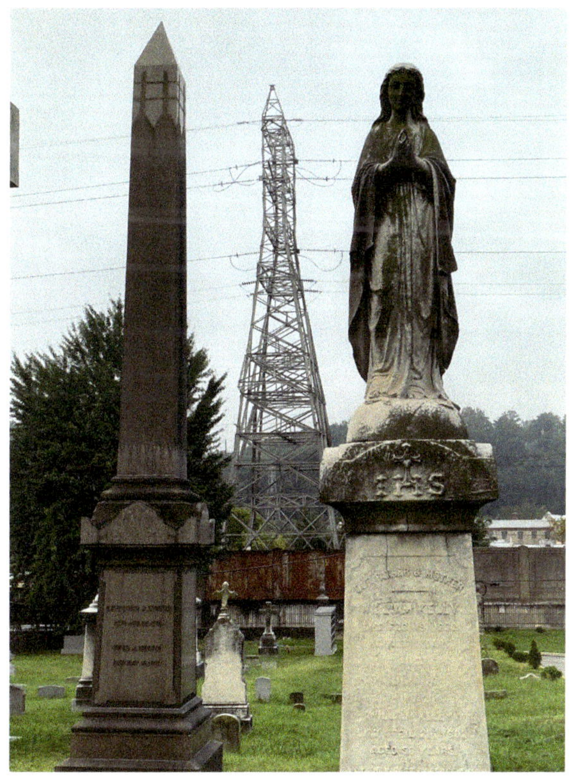

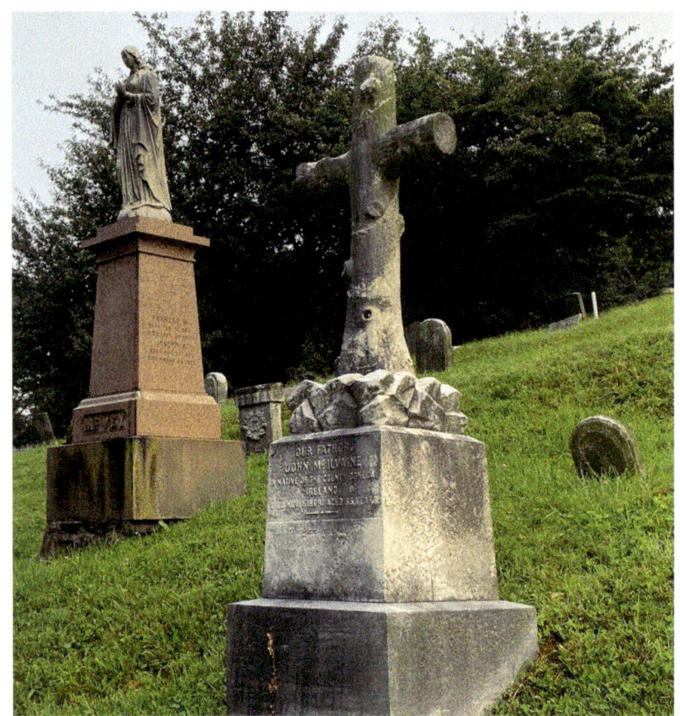

*Left:* One can just imagine how hard burials on such an incline must have been, and it's amazing that these large monuments at the apex of the hill have not slid or toppled down.

*Below:* The Roxborough Presbyterian Church seems to have been founded in the 1830s and the surrounding graveyard appears to be quite full.

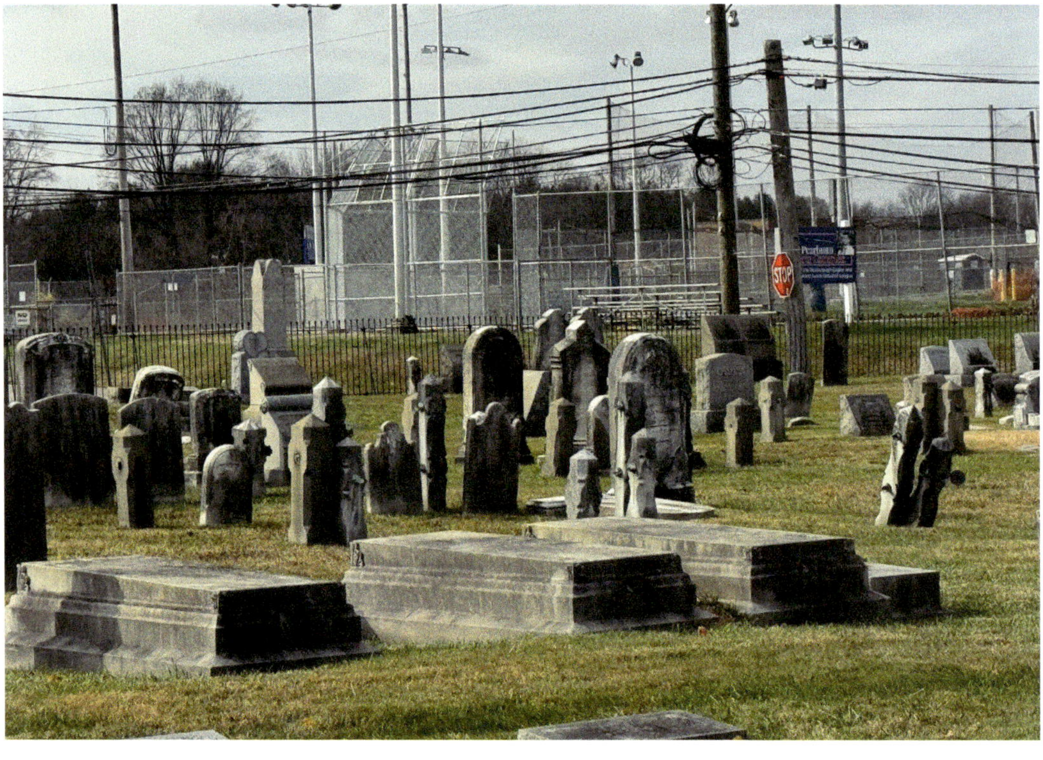

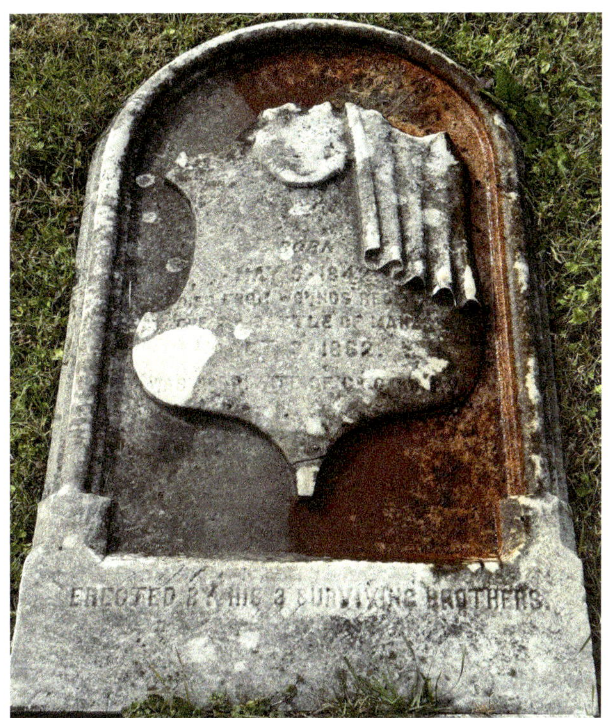


What was once likely a quaint churchyard has many toppled monuments and others needing repair or conservation, a plight similar to many of Philadelphia's oldest burial grounds.

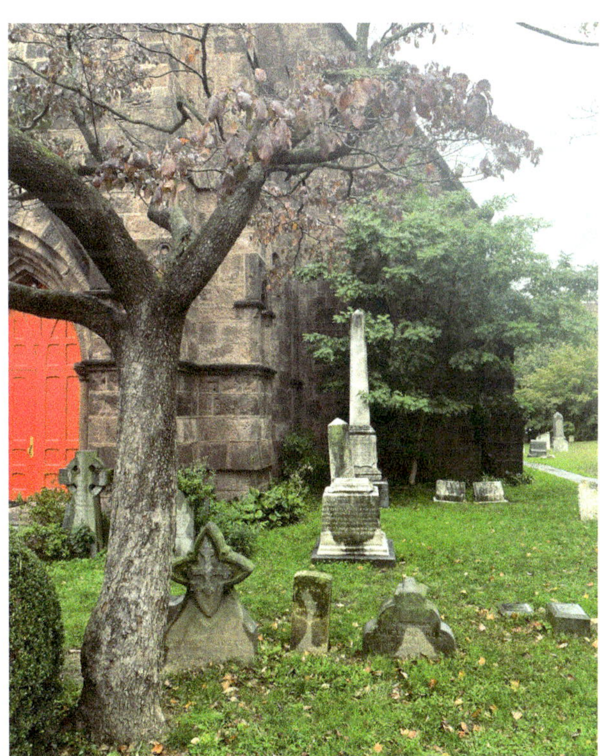

St. David's Episcopal Churchyard, also located in the Manayunk neighborhood, appears to have 1,000 or so burials, with a number of them flush with the church building that was erected in 1881 after the original 1835 building was destroyed by fire.

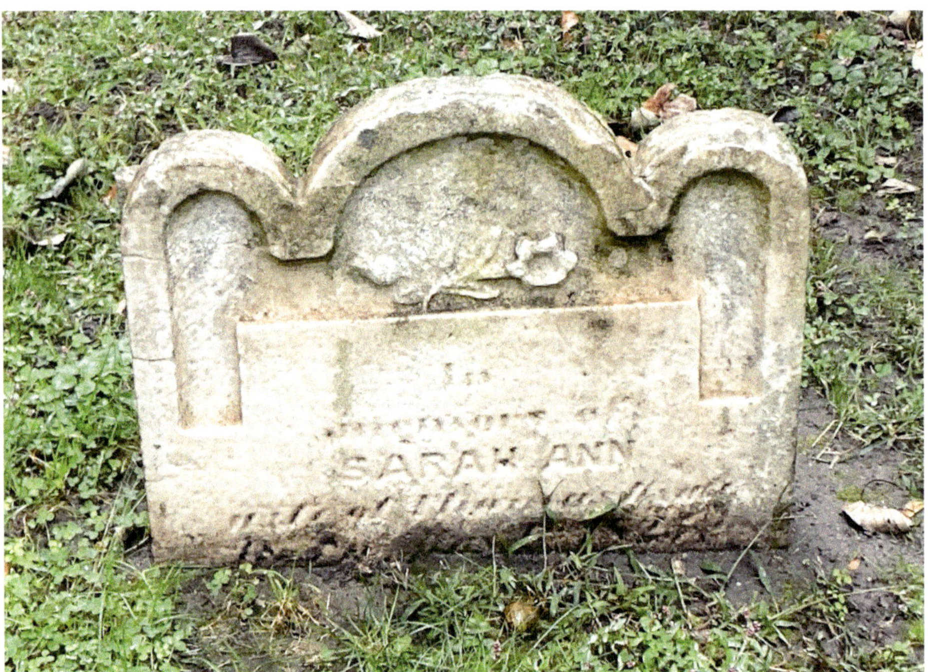

The fenced churchyard is apparently popular with neighborhood dog walkers, and it's clear that the burial grounds are not given much more attention, as evidenced by Sarah Ann's gravestone, which has sunk a few feet into the ground.

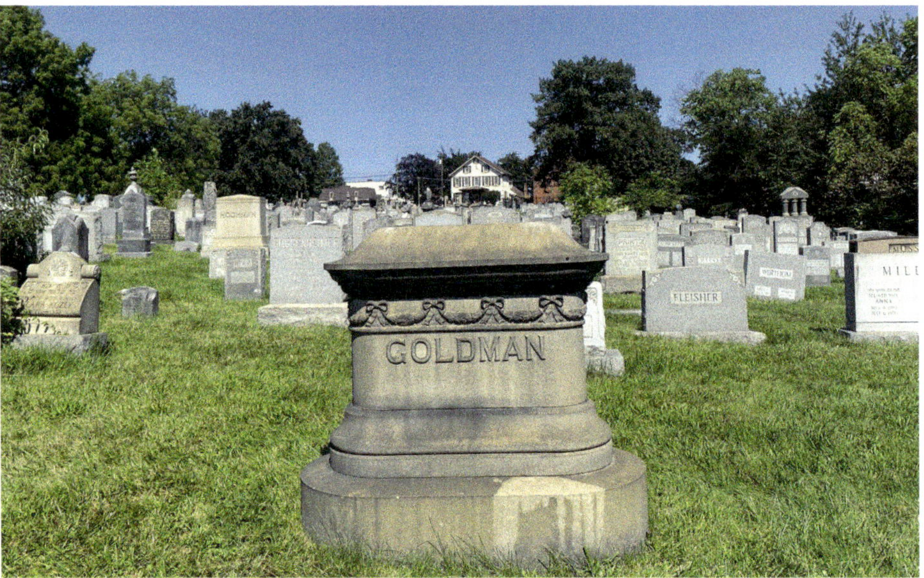

Mt Carmel Cemetery was established around 1832 to serve the Russian Jewish population in the city and received global attention in 2017 when vandals knocked over and defaced nearly 300 monuments.

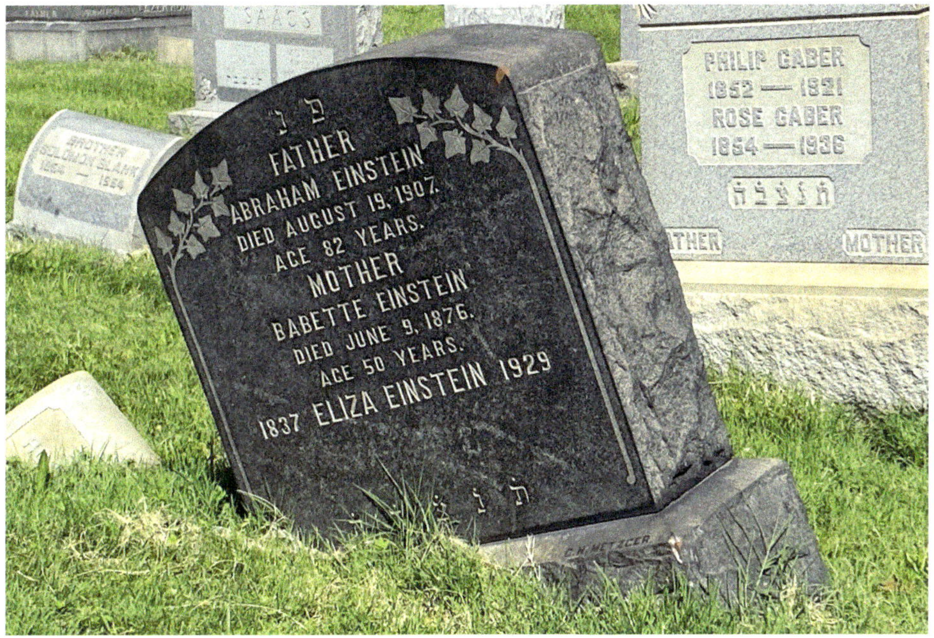

Despite fundraising efforts and many stones being reset, this tightly packed cemetery still has many listing, unstable monuments due to the lack of care over many decades.

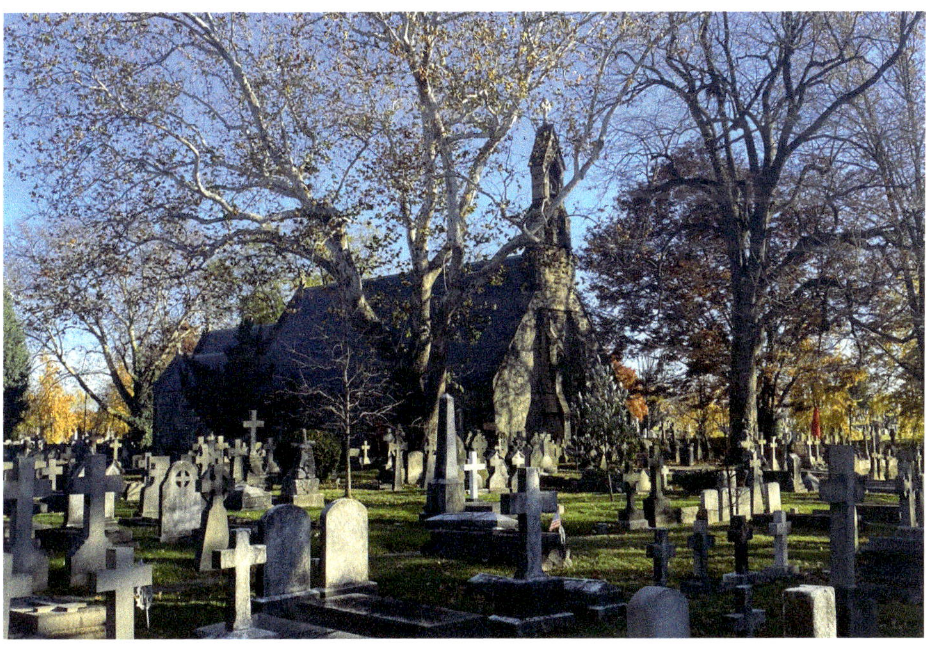

The churchyard of Saint James the Less is perhaps one of the finest burial places in the city. The Gothic-style Episcopalian church is surrounded by mature trees, and it seems every inch of ground contains interments.

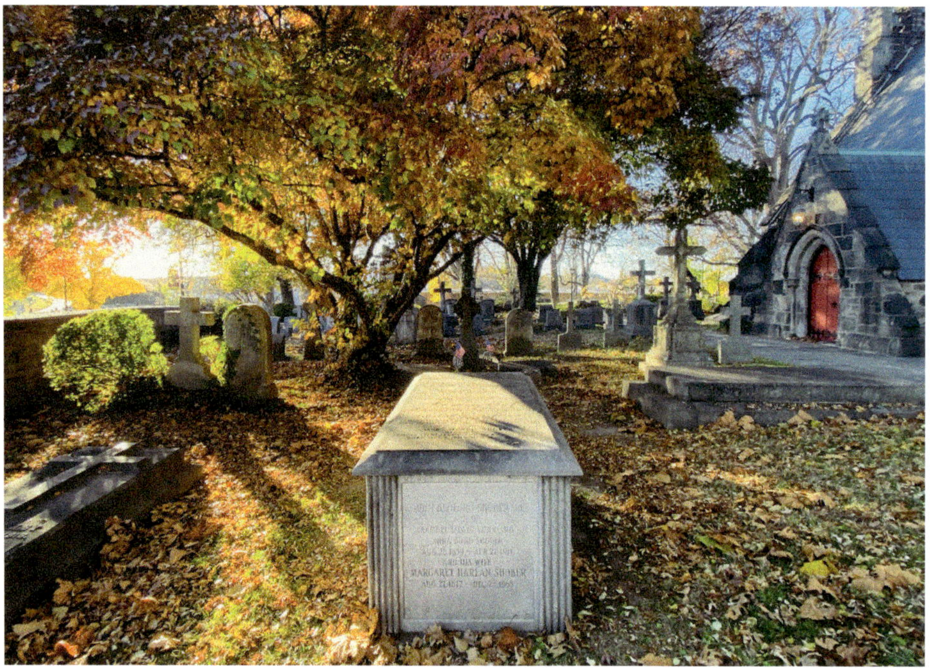

The serene setting, raised up on a small hill above street level, almost disguises the hustle and bustle of the urban environment and the fast-paced traffic on W. Hunting Park Ave.

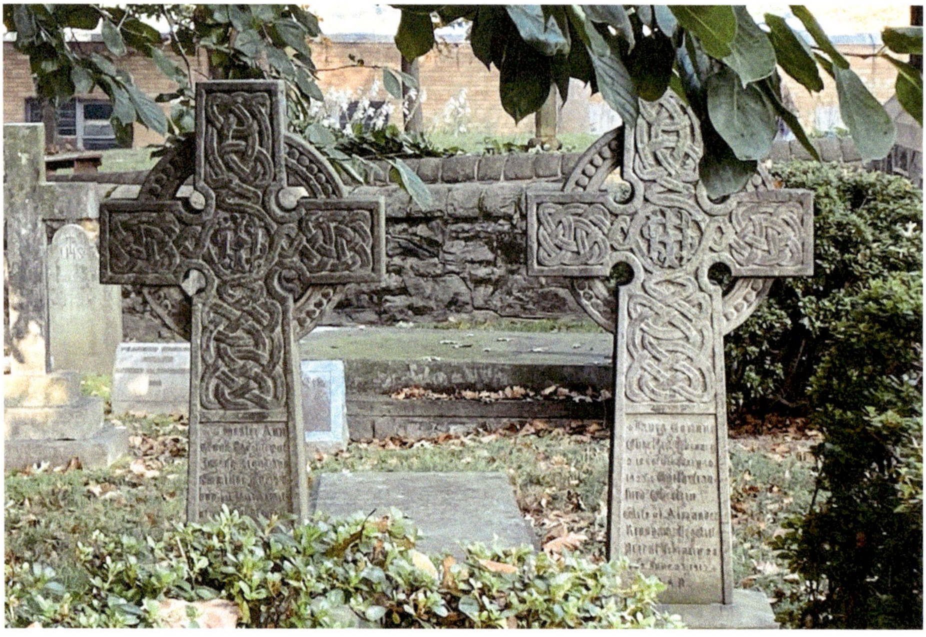

The burial grounds contain a wide variety of monuments with simple, or intricate, crosses that blend with the tree canopy and other vegetation.

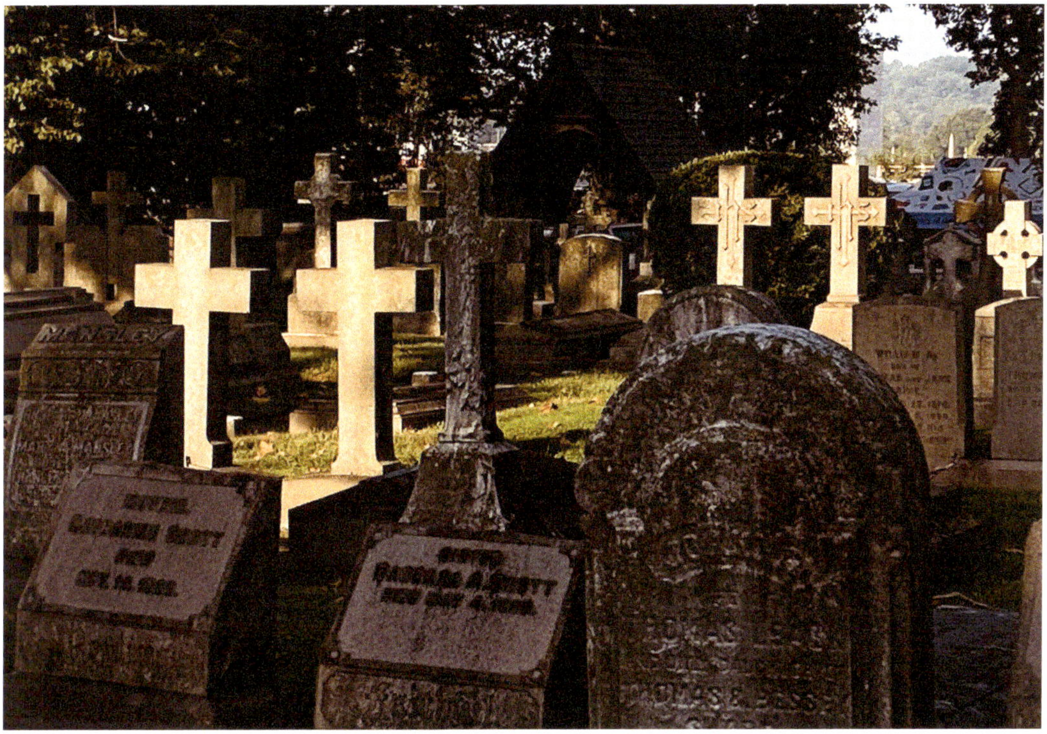

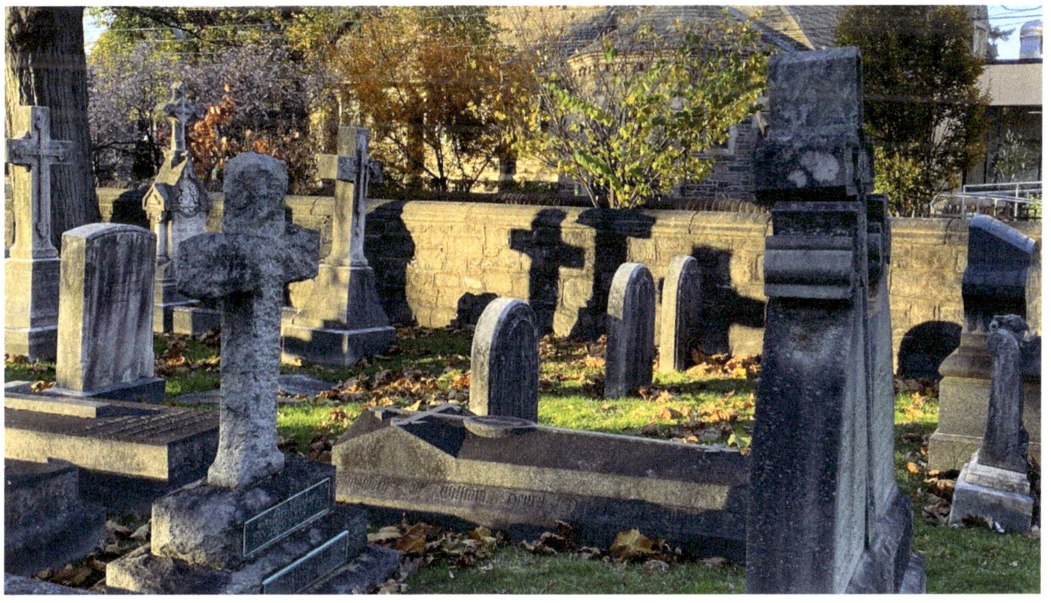

In the afternoon, the sun breaks through the largest trees to create dazzling beams of light that enhance the ambiance of the churchyard.

One can spend hours exploring the dense graves packed together at close quarters.

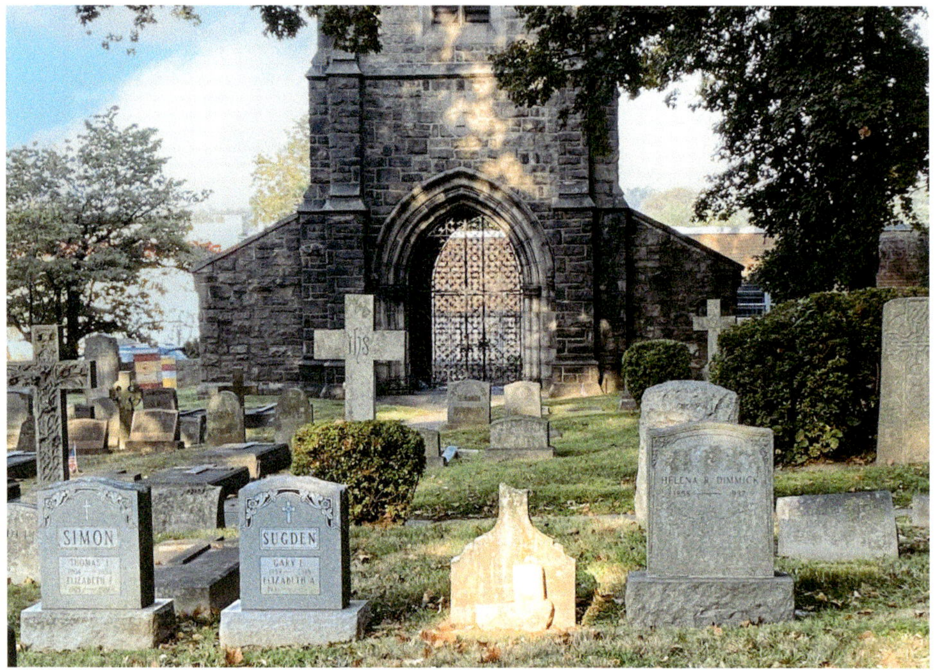

The bell tower at the rear of the churchyard houses the remains of the well-known Philadelphia merchants the Wanamakers, owners of one of the first department stores in the United States.

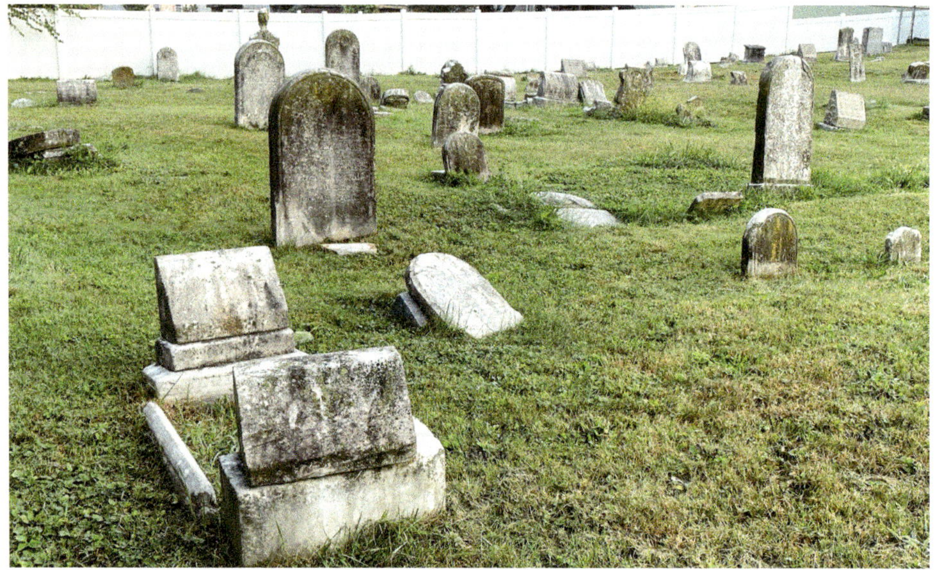

The Bethany Lutheran German Cemetery in the Manayunk neighborhood is surrounded on three sides by houses and doesn't appear to have had any burial for the past sixty-to-seventy years. While the grass is mowed, the gravestones are fading away with time.

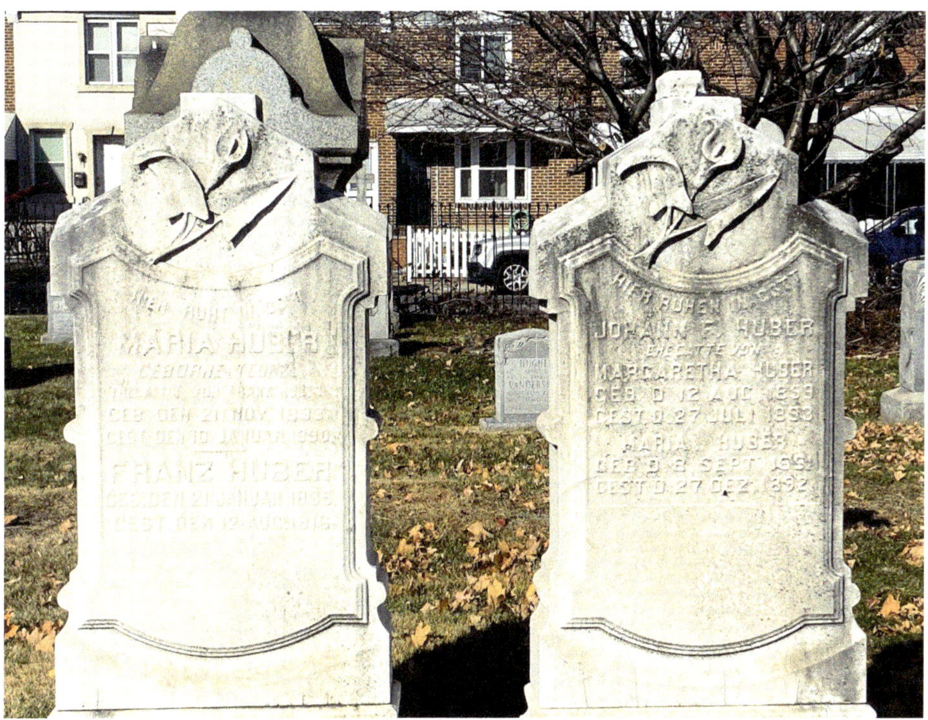

*Above:* Beginning around 1850, German Catholics were buried in a small tract that at the time was just outside city limits as the original Saint Peter's churchyard filled. Today, Saint Peter's Cemetery in Port Richmond encompasses an entire city block. It appears to be still active, although not exclusively serving a German population as the neighborhood has changed.

*Right:* Although the cemetery does not contain many grandiose monuments, there are a small number of weathered statues that have held up against the elements quite well.

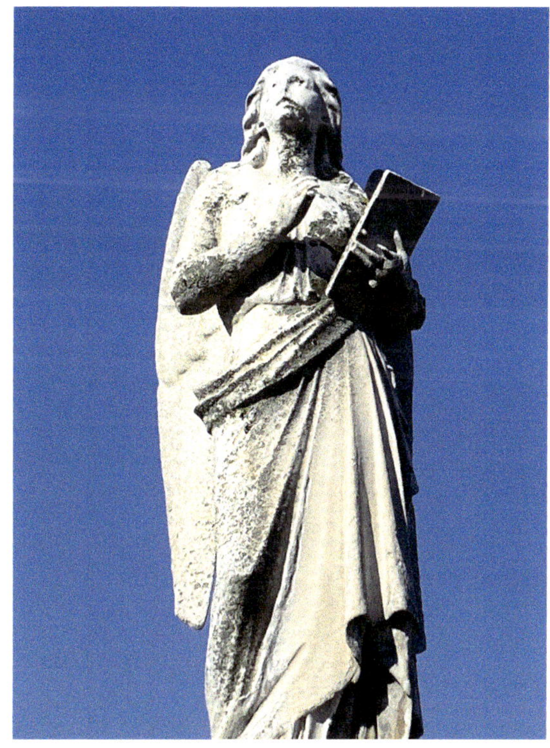

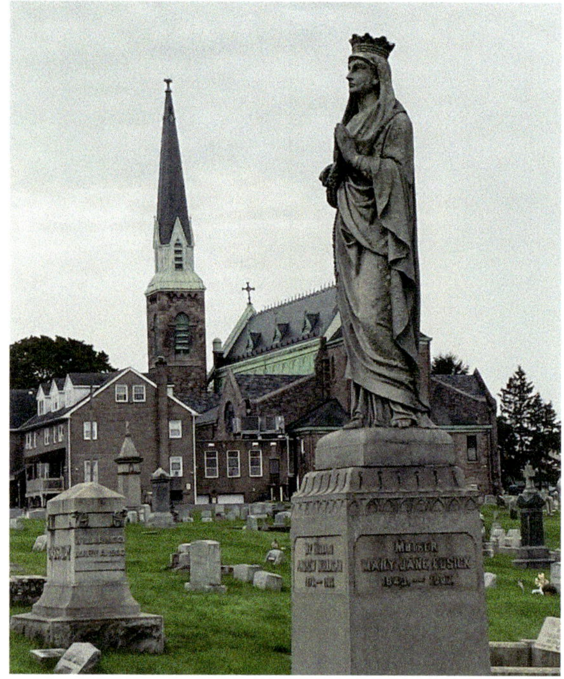

Saint Dominic Roman Catholic Church Cemetery is located in Northeast Philadelphia and contains neat, orderly rows of graves, both old and new.

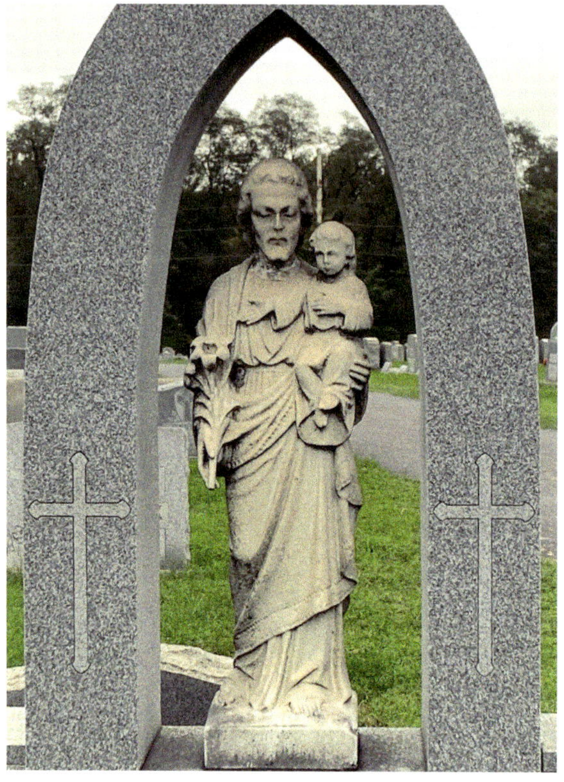

As one might expect at a Catholic cemetery, there are quite a few religious statues on top of headstones, although most are only a few feet tall.

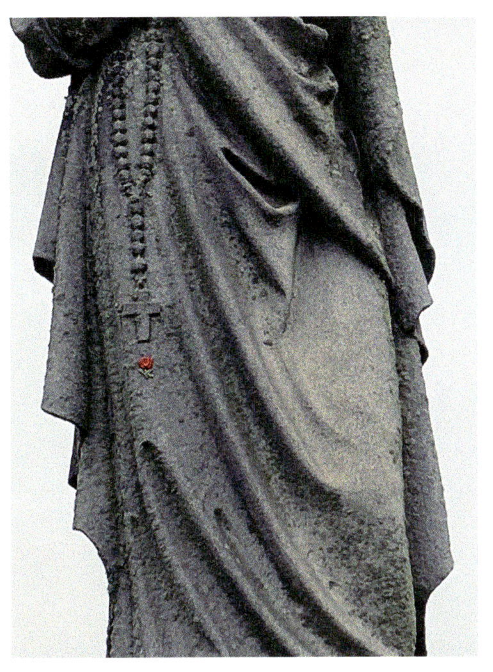

*Right:* This statue atop the Cusick-Mulligan family headstone has a beautifully hued floral inlay below the carved rosary. This small pop of color stands in stark contrast to the dull gray of the stone.

*Below:* The porcelain portrait of Pasqualina Tudisco (1878-1937) is an exciting glimpse into the past. These portraits may be the only remaining photographed evidence of one's ancestors.

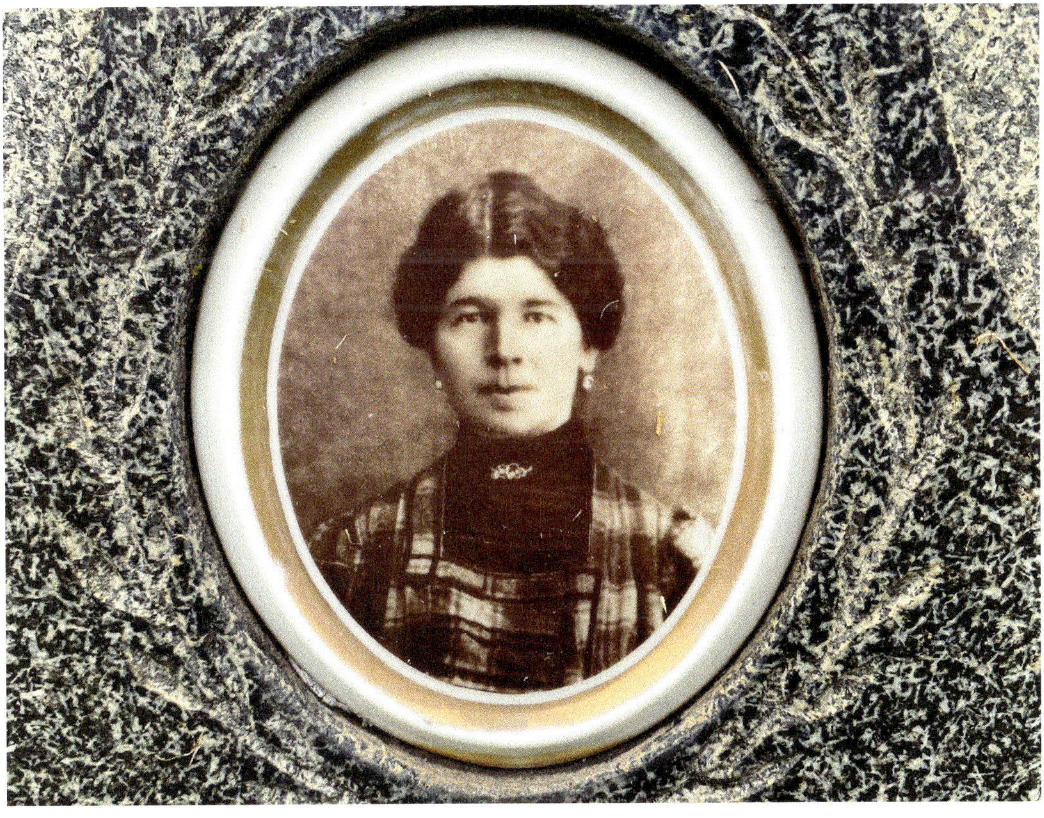

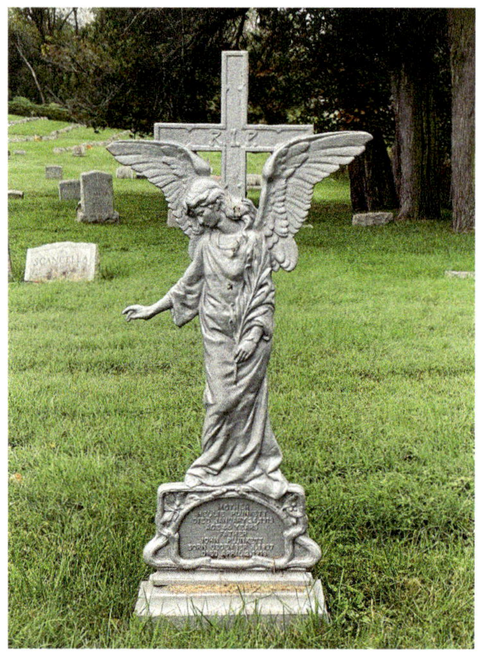

*Left:* Not to be confused with white bronze monuments, which are hollow, many cemeteries in Philadelphia include at least a small number of cast iron markers. This one appears to have been painted silver, which makes it stand out from a distance.

*Below:* The Mikveh Israel Cemetery #2 on Federal Street is another example of congregations seeking additional burial grounds in more spacious areas of the city from their original locations.

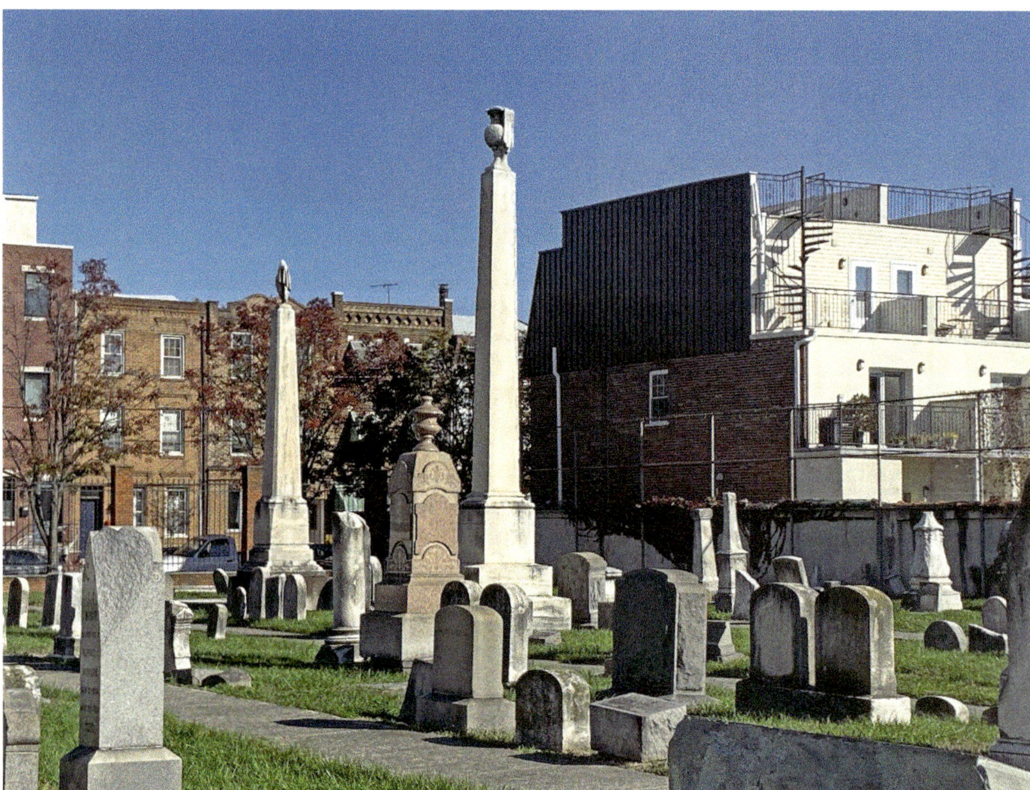

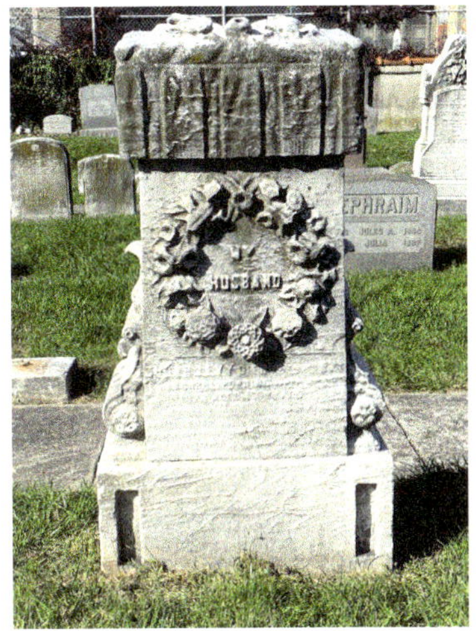

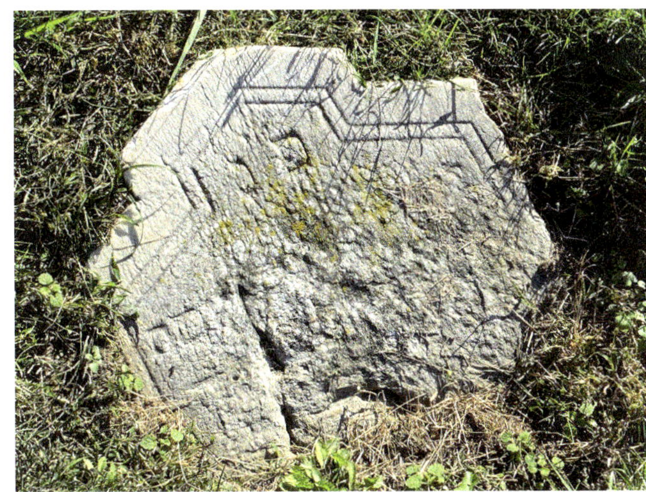

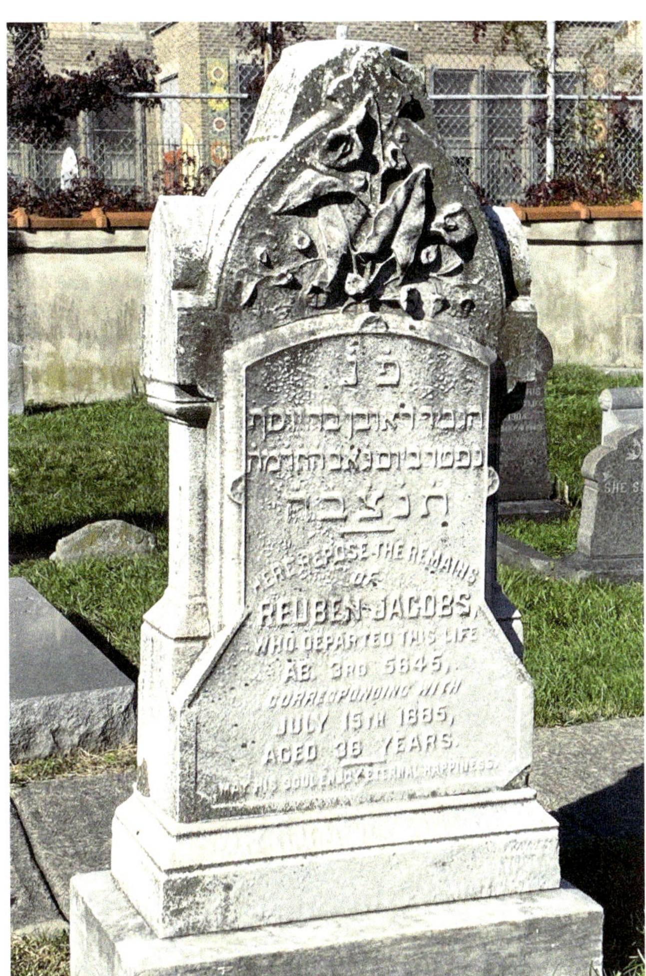

*Above left:* Established in 1849, many of the older gravestones have weathered to the point of being unreadable, but there's a certain beauty in the decay.

*Above right:* Toppled headstones will eventually be reclaimed by the ground and sink into oblivion.

*Right:* Although not ostentatious, Mikveh Israel #2 still contains many fine examples of gravestone craftsmanship.

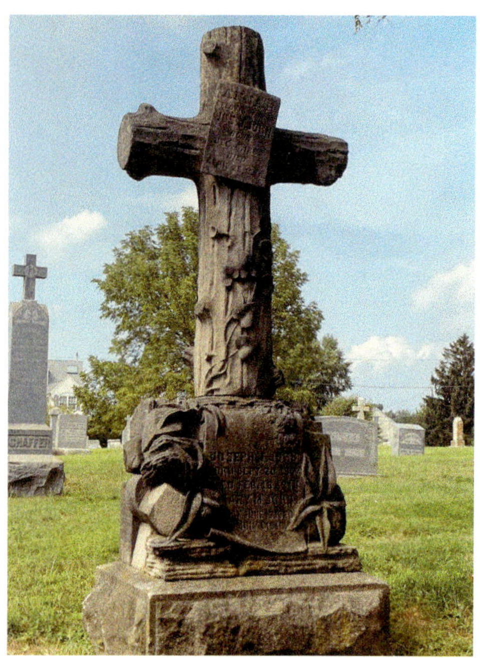

*Left:* Saint Mary of the Assumption cemetery and the related church both seem to have been closed within the last decade. This beautiful gravestone for Anna, Joseph, and Mary John can be seen from street level.

*Below:* Cathedral Cemetery in West Philadelphia is the oldest surviving archdiocese cemetery, established in 1849. It's extremely large, holding a few hundred thousand burials and has some of the finest examples of large obelisks, statuary, and unique monuments anywhere in the city.

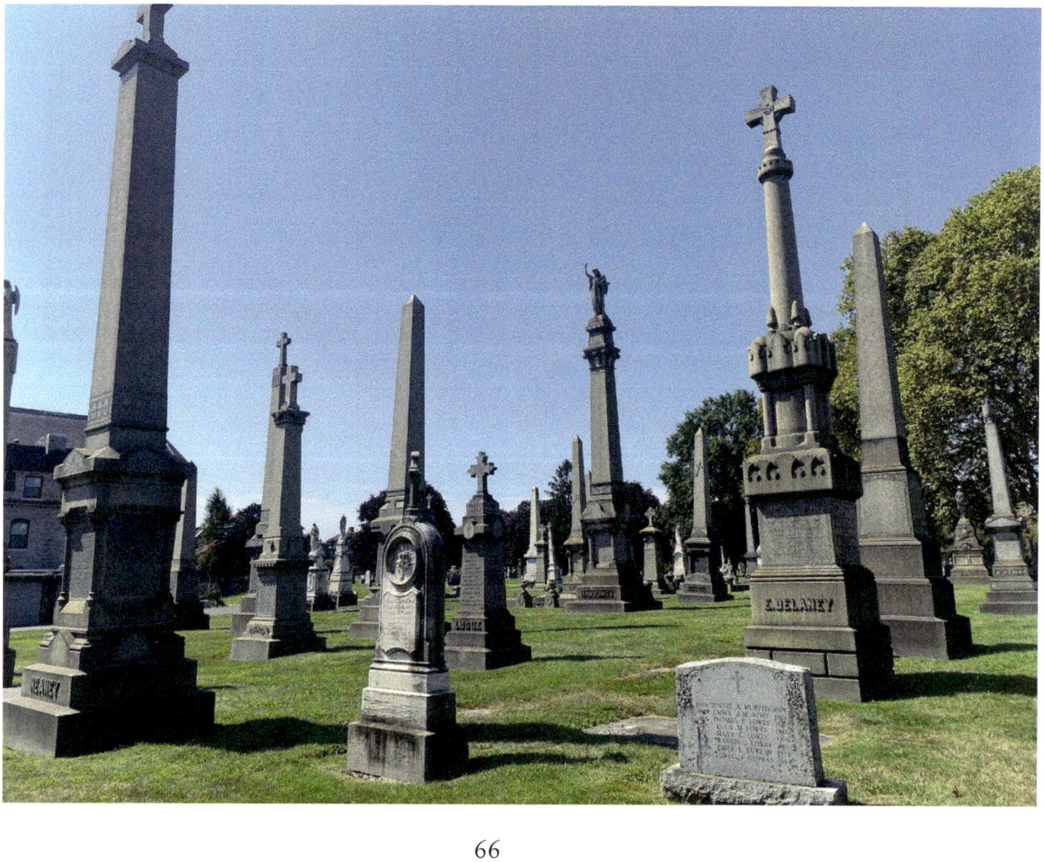

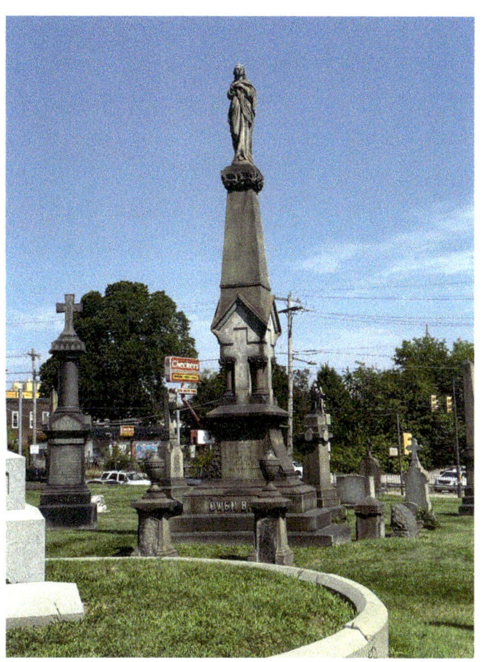

*Right:* The section in the front of the cemetery, closest to the busy intersection of Lancaster and Girard, contains large monuments to what were certainly some of the wealthiest parishioners. One wonders what this area looked like long before there was an abandoned fast-food chain across the street.

*Below:* The monument to Mary Adele HIrst (1823-1859) has exceptional details, including claw feet holding a sarcophagus, winged cherubs on each corner, and a gracious statue on top.

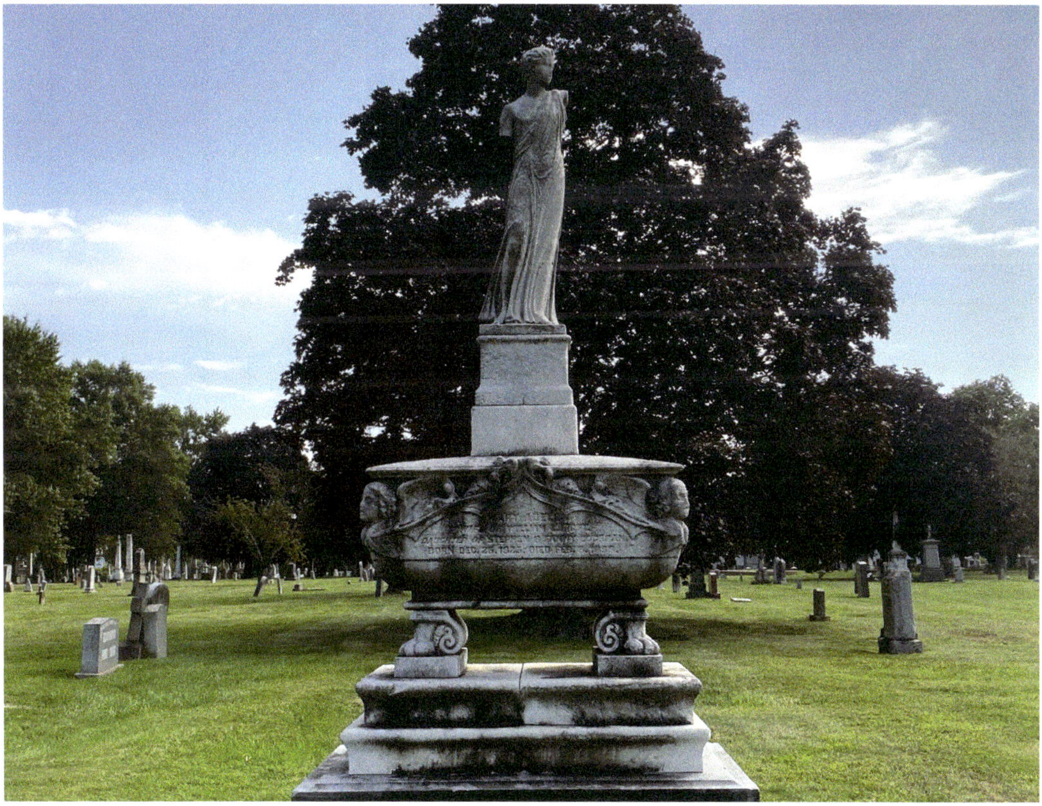

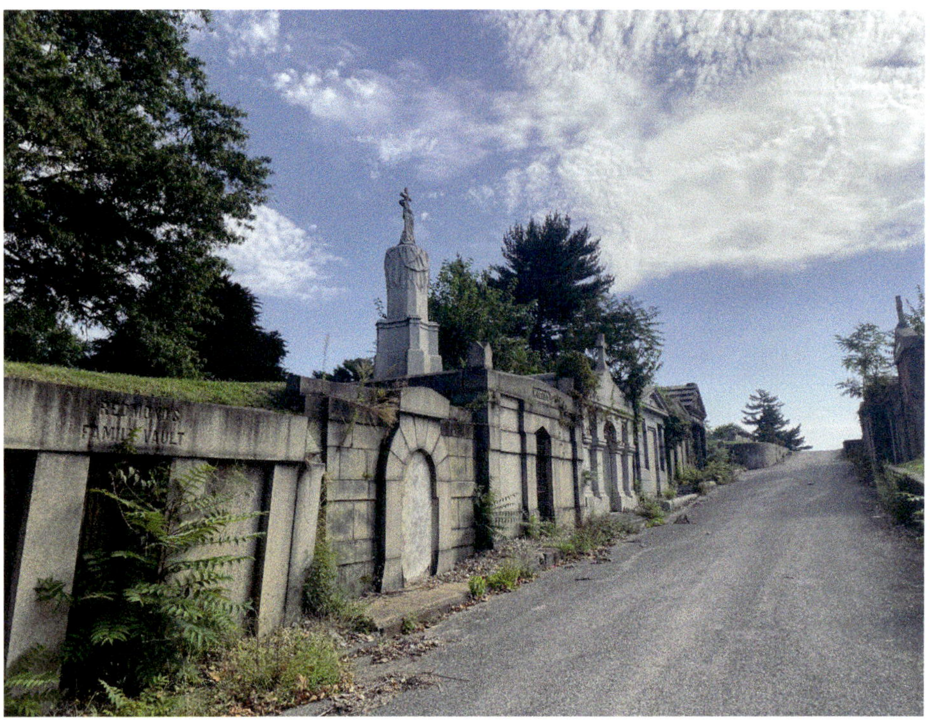

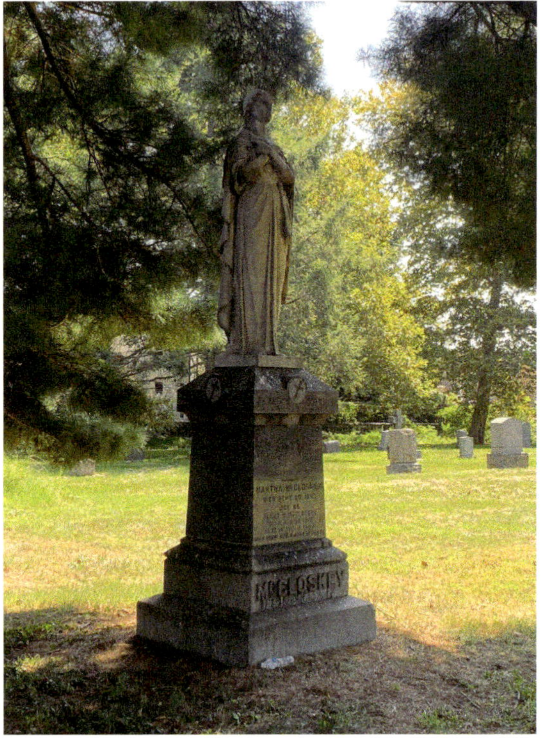

*Above:* The back corner of the property contains a row of dilapidated family vaults embedded into a hillside along the road.

*Left:* Across Wyalusing Street from the main property is a separate block that is also part of Cathedral Cemetery. It's not clear whether this annex was added at a later date, but it's perhaps the most peaceful spot on the property and features some lovely statuary.

4

# THE POST RURALS

From around 1850 through the early 1860s, Philadelphia had another small group of cemeteries established in a variety of neighborhoods, including William Penn Cemetery in the Somerton section of the far northeastern edge of the city to the nearly forgotten Hebrew Mutual, a tiny one-acre plot tucked behind the sprawling Mount Moriah in Southwest Philadelphia. Hebrew Mutual is enclosed behind a group of row houses and is only accessible from an unlabeled side alley, so many of the keenest cemetery explorers likely do not know it's there.

There were only a few churchyards founded during this period, including Emmanuel Resurrection Episcopal Church Cemetery in Holmesburg and St. Timothy's Episcopal Church Cemetery in Roxborough. Although churches were still being established, it appears it became less common for religious communities to also purchase land to set aside as a burial ground for congregants. The congregation of Adath Jeshurun, a synagogue which appears to have moved locations a few times throughout its history, established its cemetery in the Frankford neighborhood in 1863 directly adjacent to the slightly larger and older Mt. Sinai Cemetery.

The early 1860s are also the point in Philadelphia history that the federal government established its first national cemeteries in the city. Today, there are technically three: Philadelphia National Cemetery in West Oak Lane and two contained wholly within Mount Moriah Cemetery, one in Southwest Philadelphia and one in Yeadon, PA. Philadelphia National began in multiple locations throughout the city in 1862 and was consolidated to its present location in 1885, hence its inclusion in this period, as the original burials in these various locations were primarily Civil War soldiers. At Mount Moriah, the national cemeteries were established in the 1860s as well, again, to bury deceased soldiers during the Civil War. None of these locations are accepting new burials today. If you've never visited a national cemetery, these provide a great glimpse into the regimented rows of largely lookalike headstones—an awe-inspiring site to behold.

With a few exceptions, the mid-nineteenth-century cemeteries in this chapter are perhaps the least distinct or visually interesting as the properties lack the cachet of the earliest colonials or the grandeur of the rural cemeteries. While they may not have the largest monuments, the most well-known inhabitants, or the most picturesque grounds, they contain the remains of people who certainly had an impact on the city of Philadelphia in the late nineteenth and early twentieth century. As such, the seven cemeteries in this chapter are still worthwhile to explore. In many ways, the everyday aspect is what makes all cemeteries so fascinating. Whether large or small, well known or nearly forgotten, cemeteries are a lasting reminder of those who came before. The gravestones tell the story of their lives—from simple markers for one person to family plots filled with multiple generations. Even if you are not a history buff or genealogist, let alone a taphophile, there is so much to appreciate when visiting a peaceful cemetery.

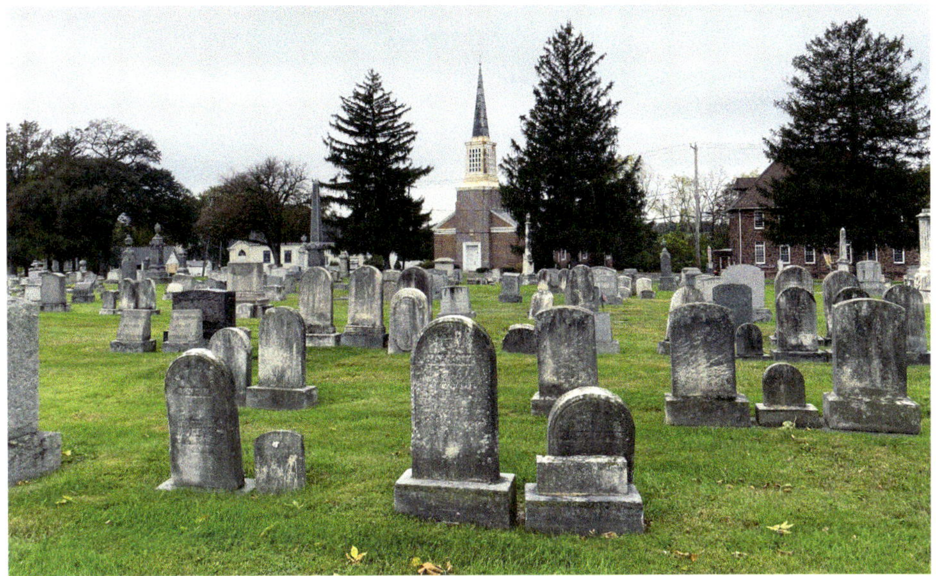

William Penn Cemetery was founded on the very edge of the city just a short distance from neighboring Bucks County in 1855. The grounds are well maintained, although it's not clear what entity manages the property.

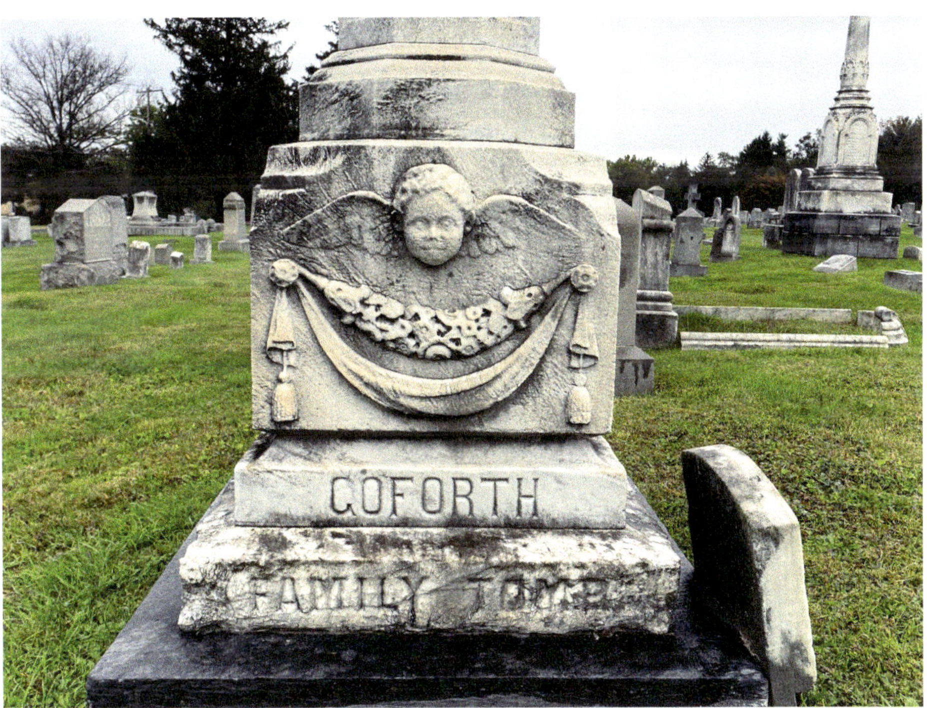

The Goforth family vault has a large obelisk erected on top that features winged cherubs and draping common on nineteenth-century monuments.

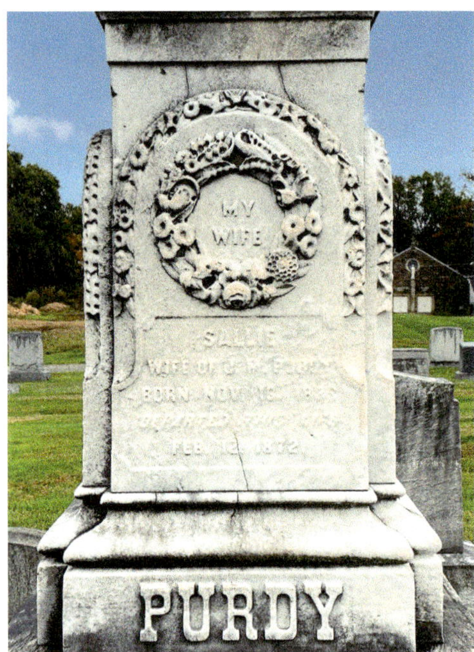

*Left:* The monument to Sallie Purdy (1836-1872) has an attractive floral wreath and edging. Although the stone is cracked and sugaring, the gravestone is still a lasting tribute to a beloved wife.

*Below:* Hazael Scott's gravestone features a hand with the index finger pointing upward toward the sky, symbolizing the deceased's reward in heaven.

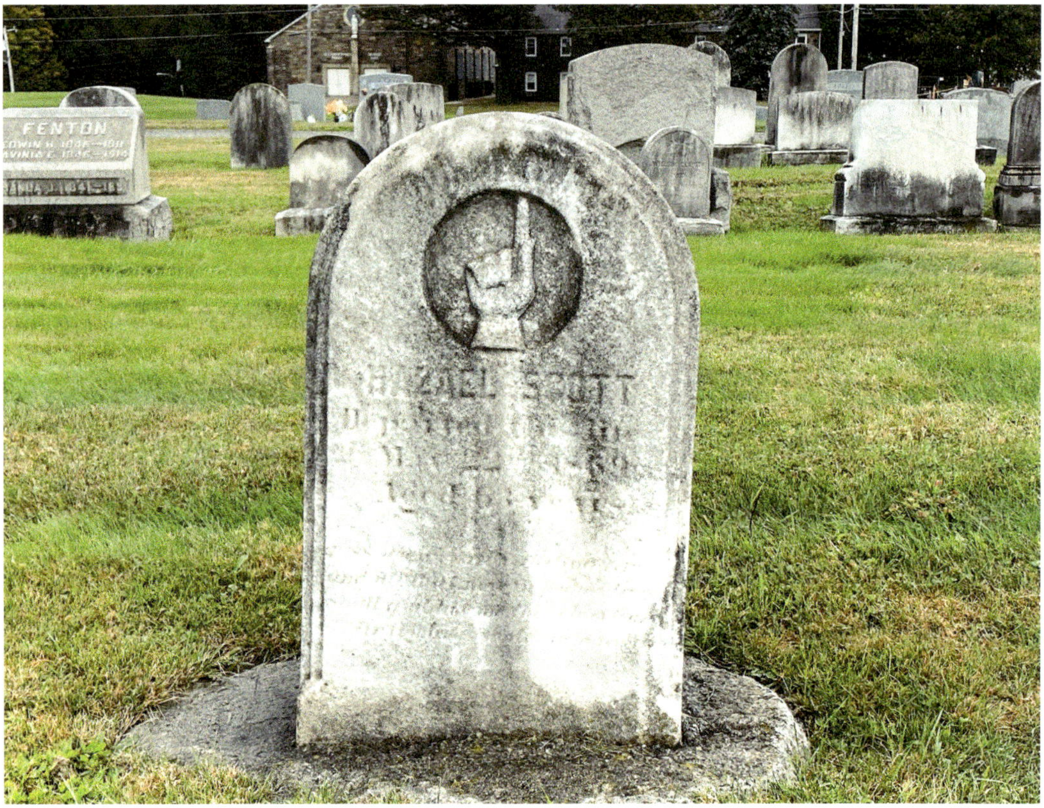

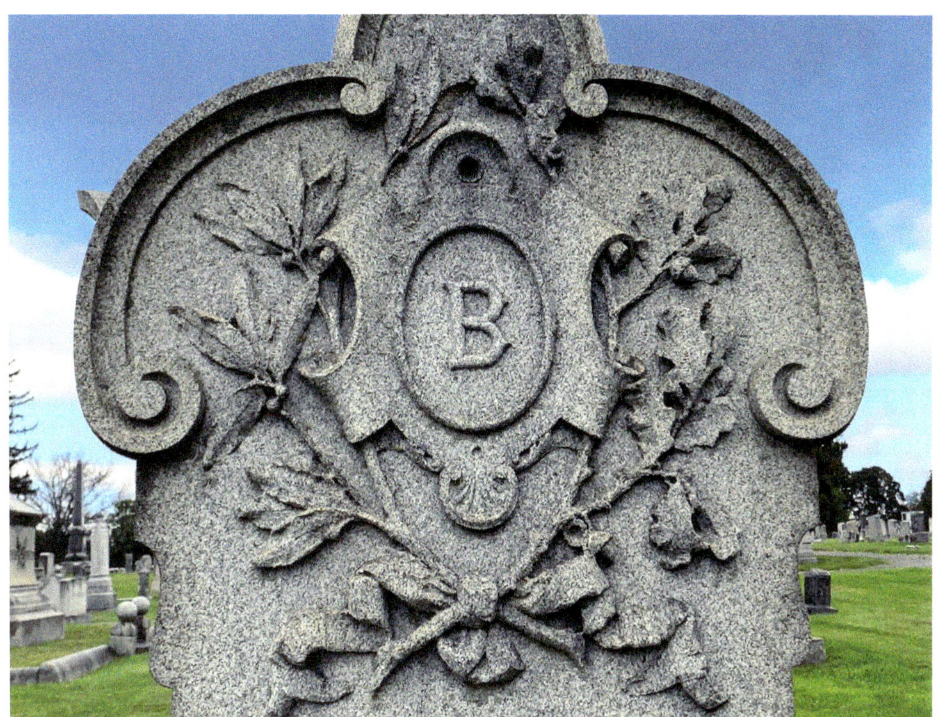

*Above:* Somewhat more modern granite gravestones are no less striking in their attention to detail.

*Right:* The B'nai Israel Burial Ground, aka Hebrew Mutual Burial Ground, is a tiny half-acre plot of ground tucked just behind Mount Moriah Cemetery in Southwest Philadelphia. Having been abandoned, at some point those seeking to save the remaining headstones moved them from individual graves to the inside edge of the property and set them in concrete, causing many to sink below their inscriptions.

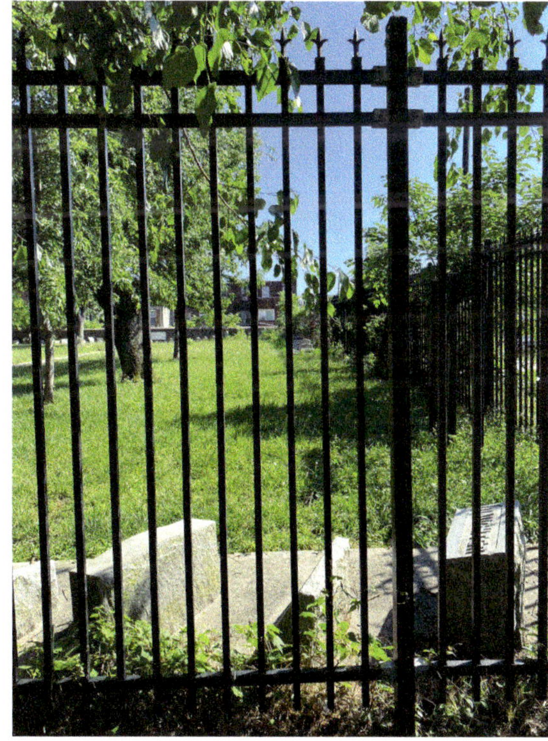

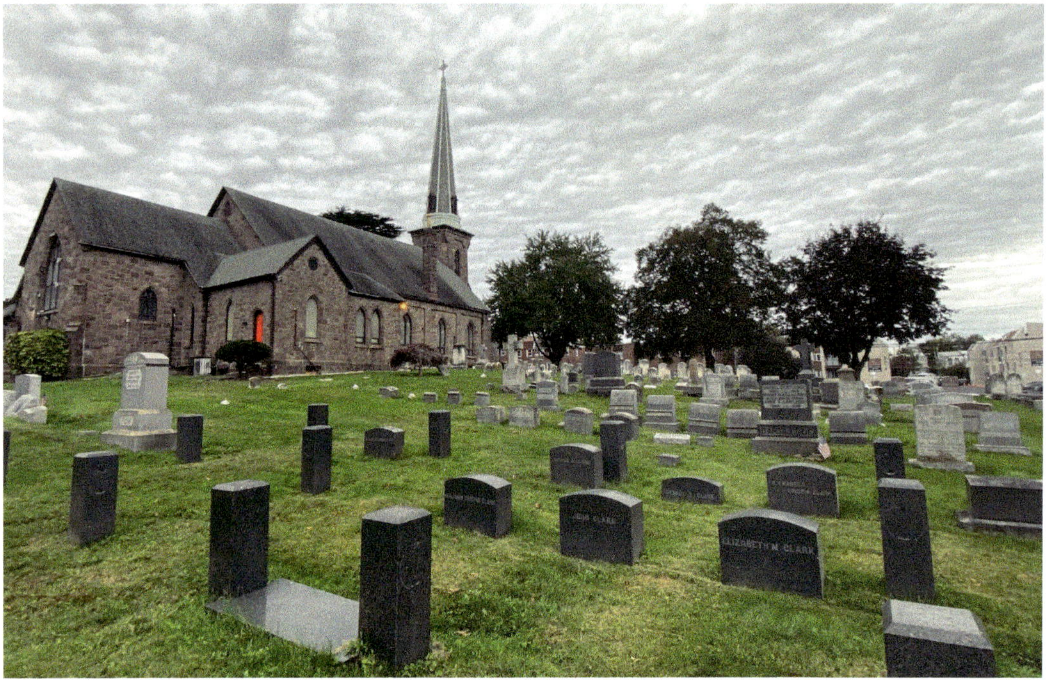

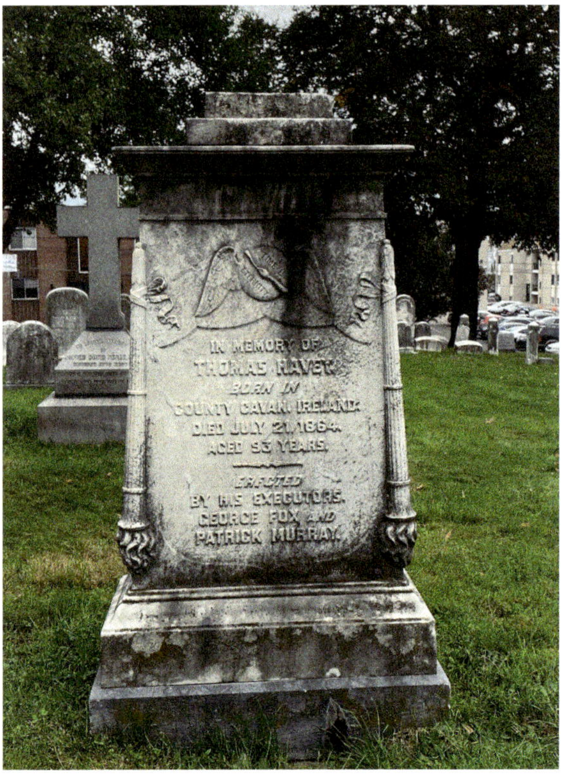

*Above:* The Emmanuel Resurrection Episcopal Cemetery in the Holmesburg section of Philadelphia prominently features a large stone worship building. The cemetery appears to have been established in the 1860s some years after the church's founding.

*Left:* One of the older monuments for Thomas Havey of Ireland, who died in 1864, features the epitaph "Time & Eternity" on the top and two upside-down torches on the sides, indicating his soul's transition to the afterlife.

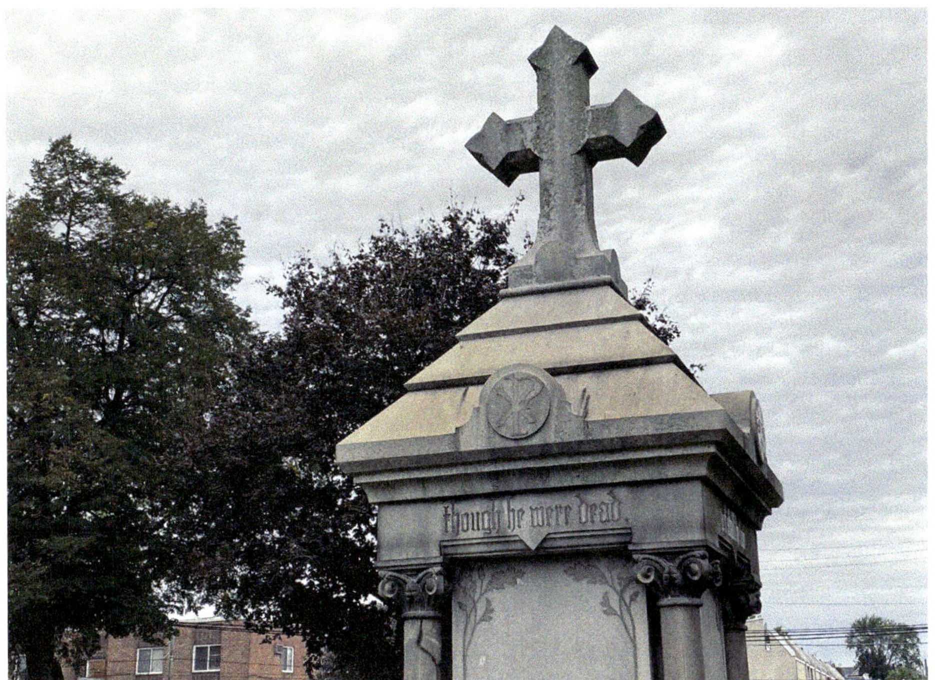

The top of this monument includes the beginning of the Biblical verse, "Though he were dead, yet shall he live."

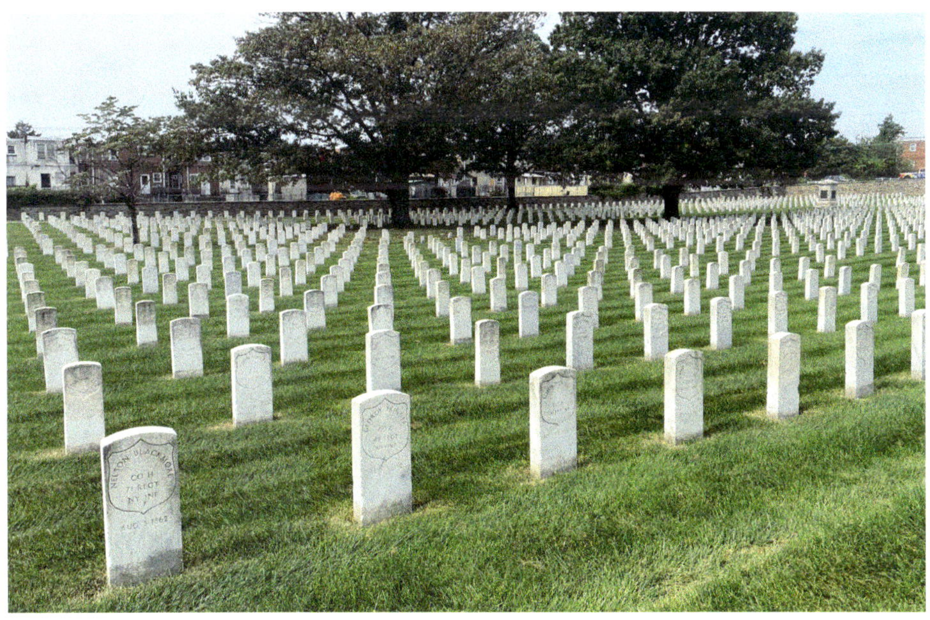

In addition to the two areas within Mount Moriah, Philadelphia National Cemetery is the only other burial space wholly dedicated to veterans. Philadelphia National began as multiple locations in 1862, with remains moved to this location in 1885.

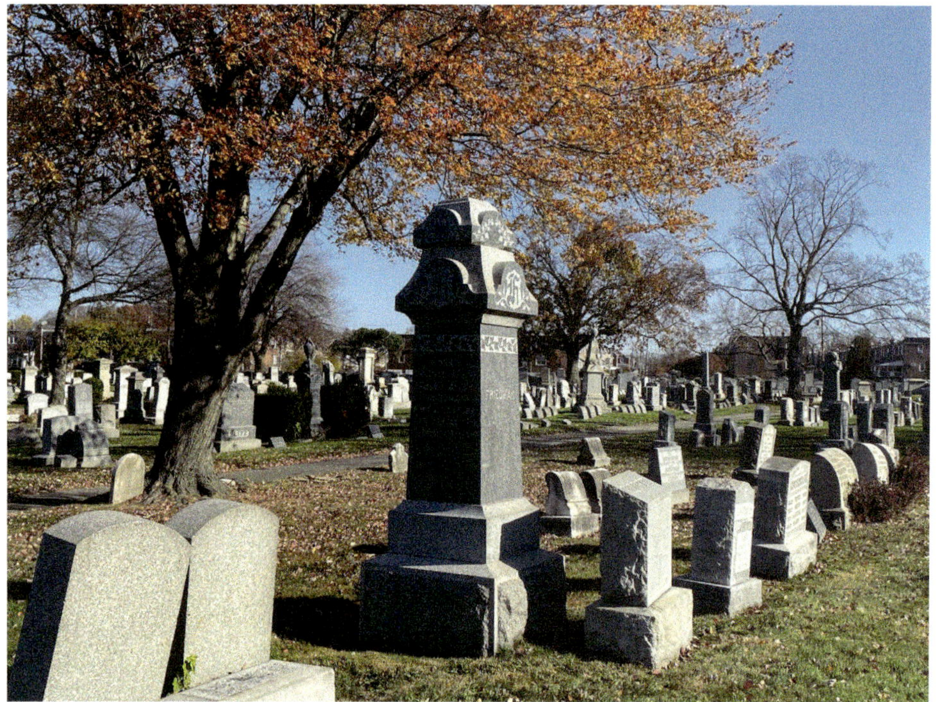

Adath Jeshurun Cemetery was established in 1861 and is directly adjacent to the slightly larger Mt. Sinai. It appears to still be active, and although the gravestones here are generally less ostentatious than its neighbor, it's still a serene resting spot.

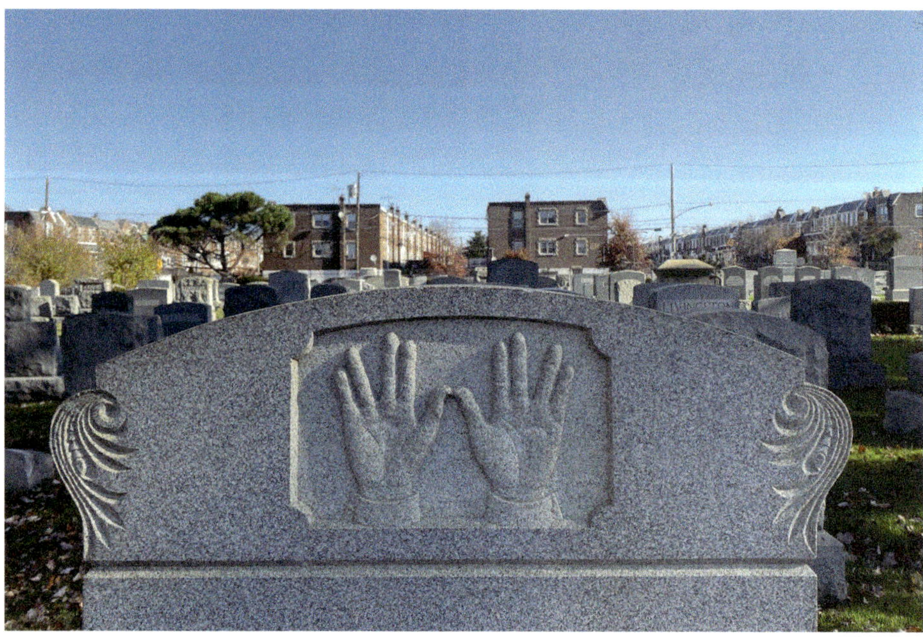

These symbols on many Jewish gravestones, both old and new, are a gesture of priestly blessing.

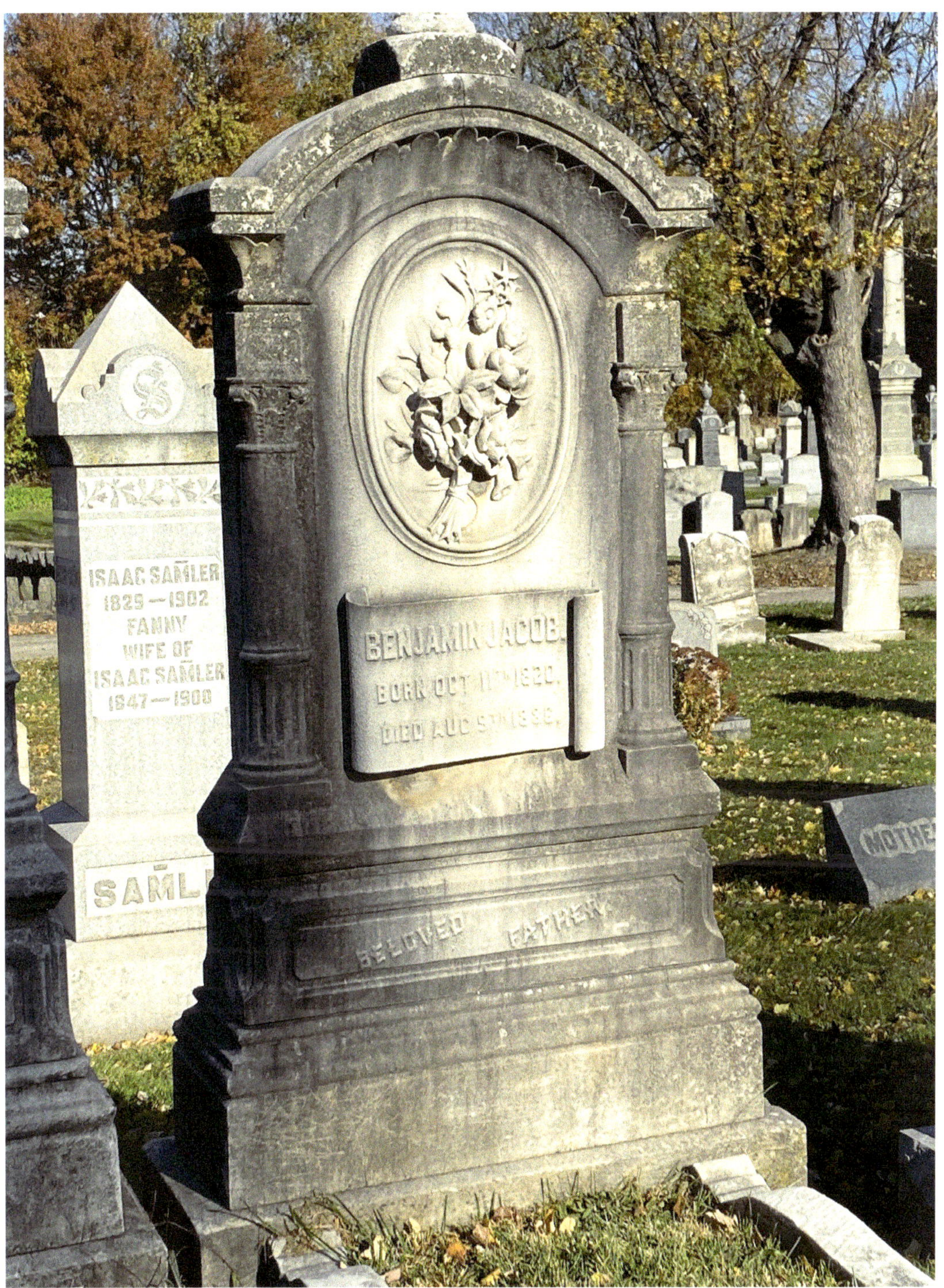

Certainly a bit less common at Jewish cemeteries, there are still a number of examples of intricately carved floral bouquets atop many of the nineteenth-century gravestones.

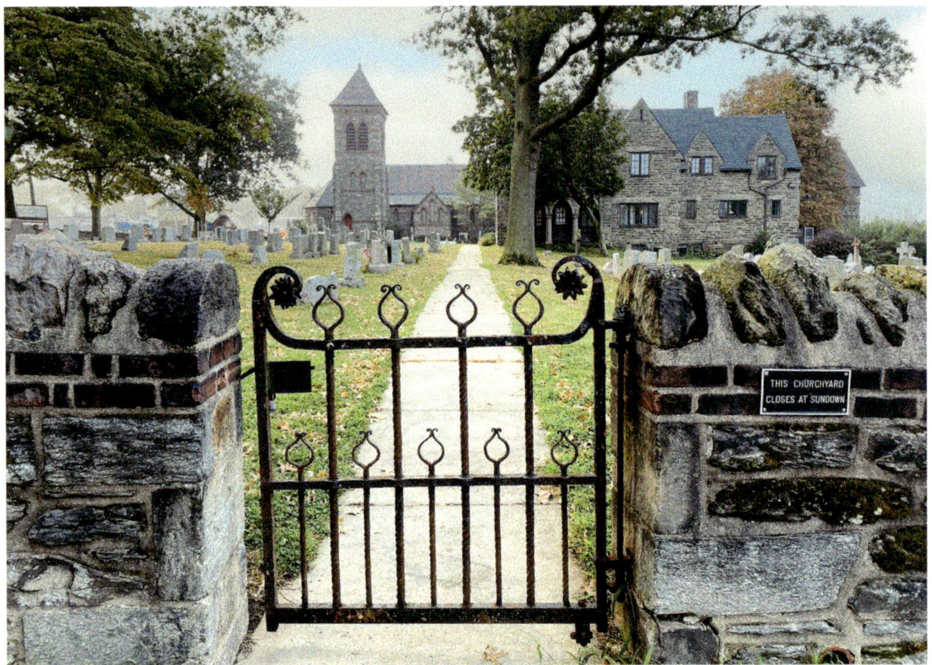

St. Timothy's Episcopal Church Cemetery in the Roxborough neighborhood of Philadelphia is surrounded by a low stone and brick wall with iron entry gates.

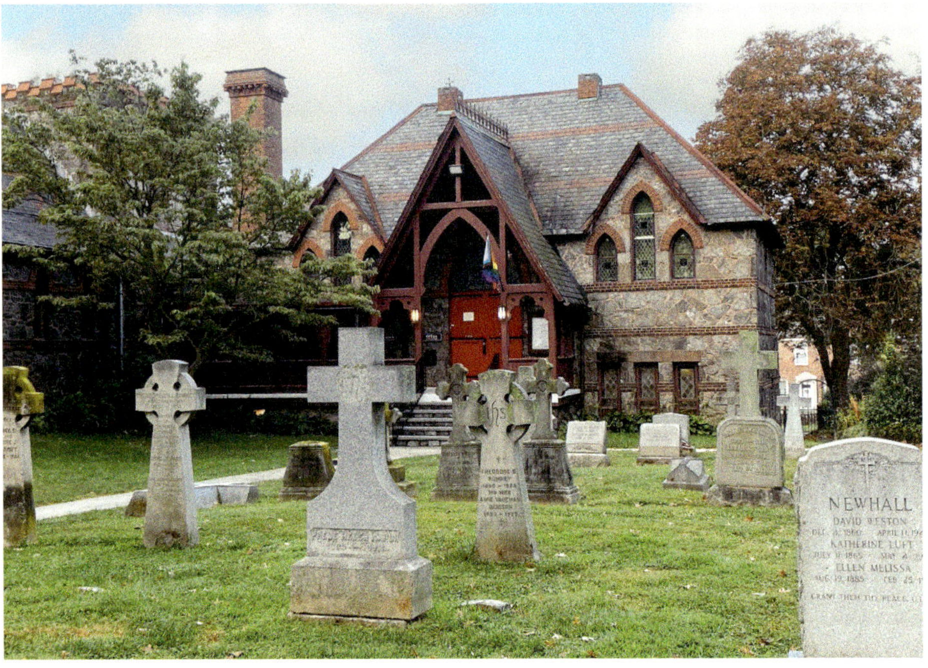

The cemetery grounds contain many traditional gravestones that are generally of a subdued nature.

# 5

# THE WANING OF THE PHILADELPHIA CEMETERY ERA

By the late nineteenth century, Philadelphia had already reached a point where many of its oldest burial grounds had become defunct as congregations dwindled or moved and sold off properties that contained their original graveyards. Although many people hold the belief that a cemetery is somehow forever and can never be utilized as anything else, Philadelphia's history shows that has never really been true. Remains were generally—but not always completely—moved to locations outside of the city. One could walk past these sites none the wiser, but that's a story for another time.

The last of Philadelphia's new cemeteries was the 1890 opening of Har Nebo, a privately-owned Jewish cemetery in the Oxford Circle area. After this point, additional burial grounds were always outside of the city limits in nearby Delaware, Bucks, or Montgomery counties. One can imagine this was due to the availability and cost of land inside of the city, as well as the flow of people to homes in the suburbs. As the city continued to be built up, reserving 50 or more acres for a burial ground seemed to have reached a point that was no longer tenable, and one would imagine at some point Philadelphia passed legislation prohibiting the establishment of new cemeteries within its borders.

In addition to Har Nebo, a second Jewish cemetery, Chevra Bikur Cholim, was opened directly adjacent to the older Adath Jeshurun and Mt. Sinai cemeteries. There were two new Catholic cemeteries established—New Cathedral and Most Holy Redeemer. Both locations were tied to predecessor sites that had filled substantially or the new burials were intended to serve a distinct neighborhood away from their mother site. The Knights of Pythias Greenwood Cemetery, not far up the road from Har Nebo, was founded to serve members of this fraternal organization and their families.

There were also some new, non-denominational cemeteries opened during this period, such as Ivy Hill, Magnolia, and Northwood. These were established a bit too late to formally be part of the rural cemetery movement, but all three are on the larger side when comparing the acreage of Philadelphia's cemeteries. All three appear to still be quite active today, likely because they have more burial space remaining due to their relatively recent age and perhaps because they are not tied to a specific religious community. Magnolia, a small and relatively non-descript location in the Tacony neighborhood, had more evidence of recent burials than any other visited.

The last of Philadelphia's cemeteries have not been spared by rapid urbanization or the struggle to stay afloat. At some point, Most Holy Redeemer lost some of its property to the city installing cross streets right through it and the rear side of the cemetery sits under the shadow of I-95, the most highly traveled highway in the country. The Knights of Pythias Greenwood Cemetery lost part of its property in a land sale and had bodies reinterred in a mass grave near the front of the grounds, while Har Nebo has struggled to keep the grass cut and monuments from toppling over. This is certainly a common theme across the eras—maintaining a cemetery includes mowing, tree care, monument care, road maintenance, and more, and often perpetual care funds established along the way are not enough on their own to fund these massive undertakings.

Of all the cemeteries in this chapter, Ivy Hill Cemetery appears to be the single site most immune from the pressures outside its gates. Established as a non-profit, non-sectarian cemetery in 1867, Ivy Hill is an exceedingly pleasant location filled with a wide variety of monuments. One finds groundskeepers here interested in stopping to chat with visitors about the history of the cemetery, and it is the perfect location for a summer picnic with plenty of spots to find some shade.

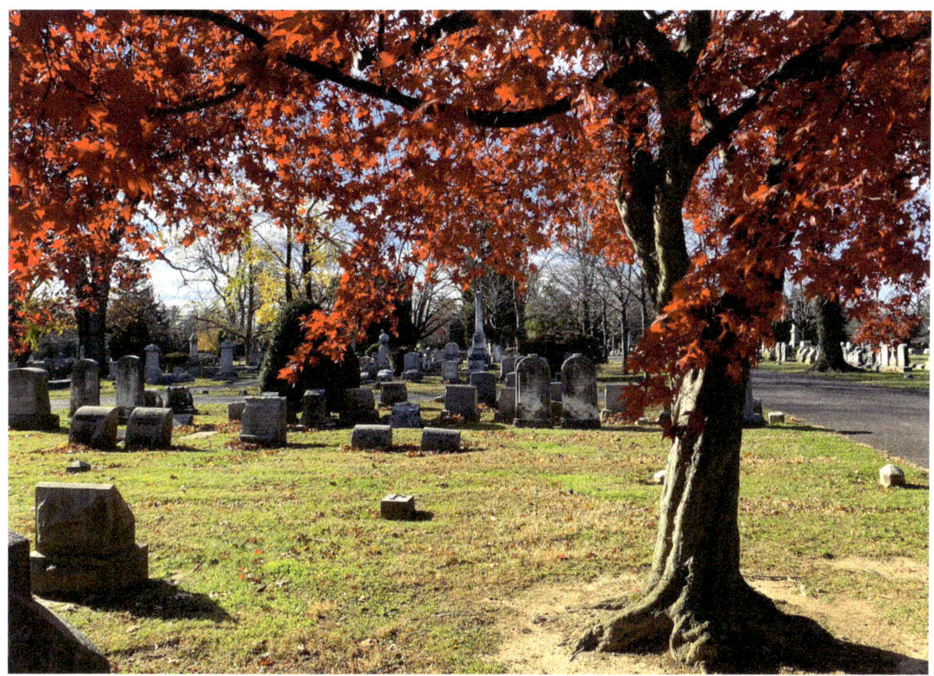

The Ivy Hill Cemetery and Crematorium was founded at the end of the 1860s and quickly became a popular burial location. Notable interments include boxer Smokin' Joe Frazier and Joni Sledge of Sister Sledge's "We Are Family" fame.

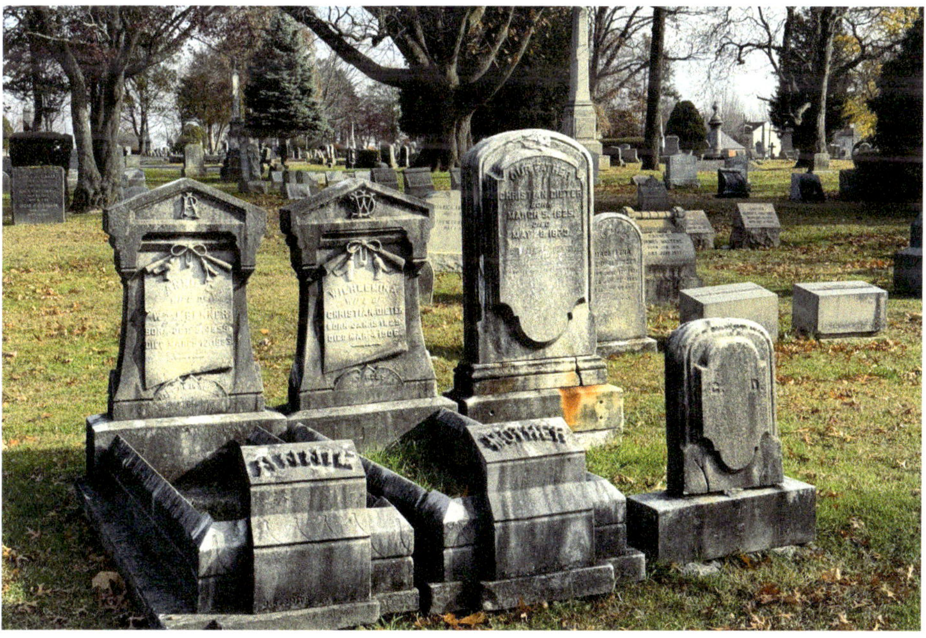

There are many nineteenth-century style family plots, featuring cradle graves, obelisks, and statuary.

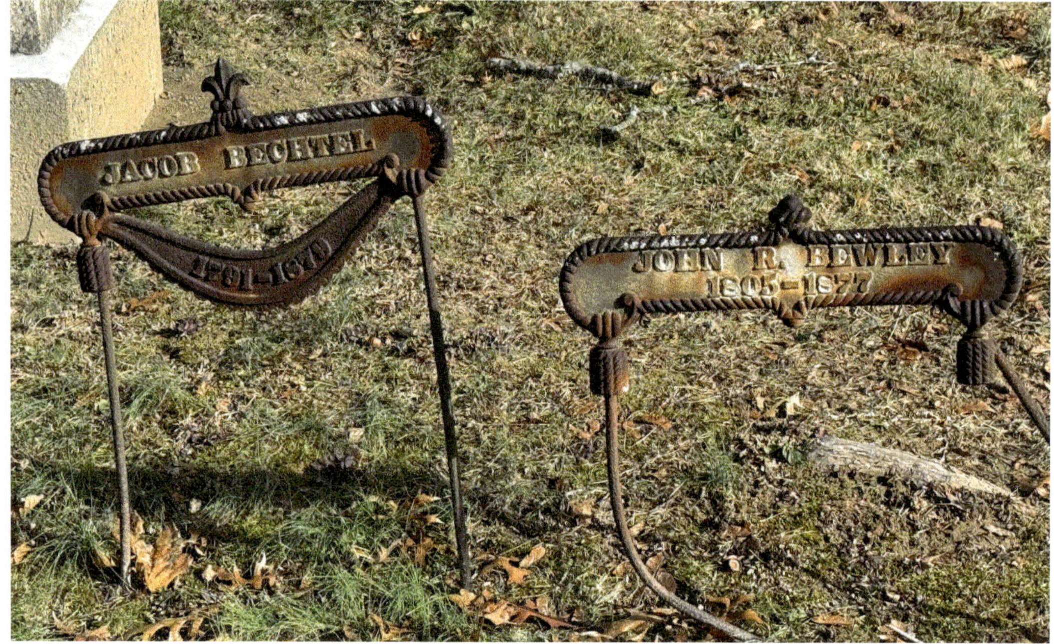


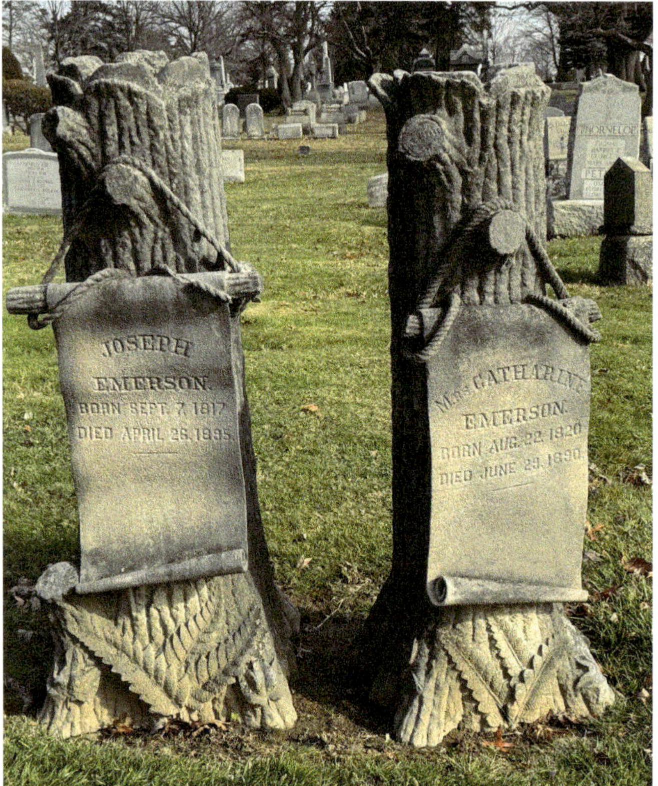


*Above:* Banner-like iron markers intended to stand above a grave on two legs with just the deceased's name along with birth and death year and sometimes an accompanying panel that reads "Mother" or "Brother" were popular in the late 1800s. They seem to have been produced locally in Philadelphia, but unfortunately many have not withstood rusting and broken pieces or simply being stolen for scrap.

*Left:* The Emersons have a pretty pair of matching tree stump tombstones with hanging, scrolled banners bearing their names and birth and death dates.

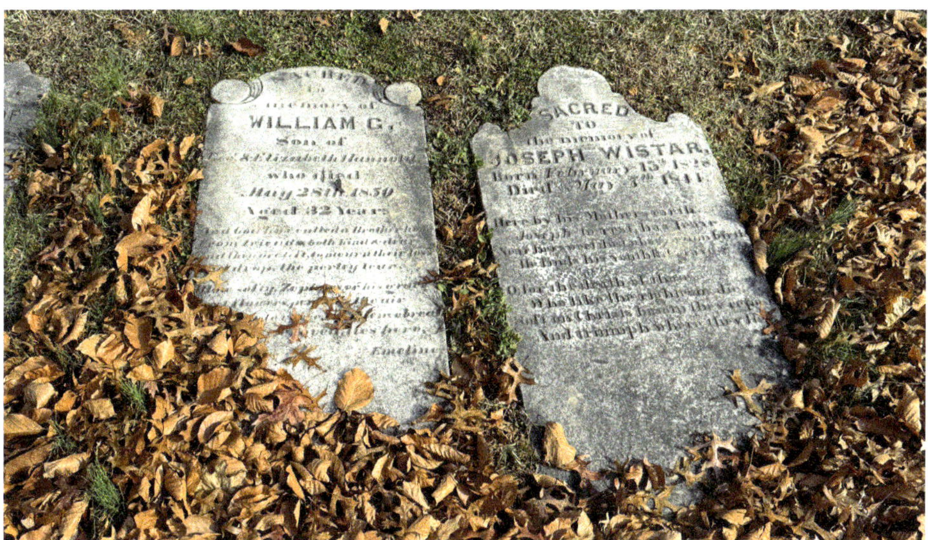

Like many larger cemeteries, Ivy Hill is home to reinterred remains from other locations throughout the city. The Second Baptist Church bought lots at this cemetery when the congregation relocated and their church and graveyard was sold.

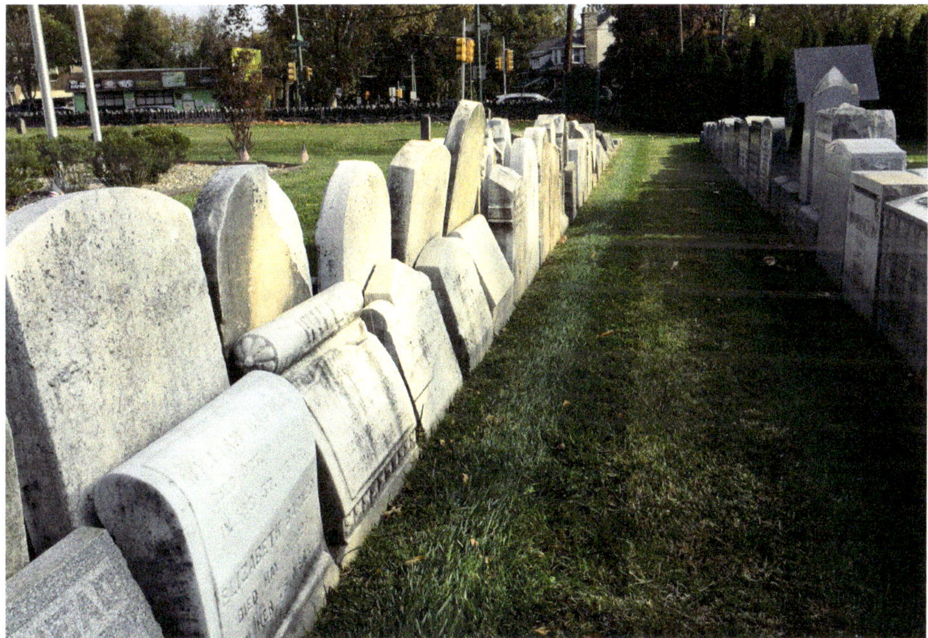

The Knights of Pythias Greenwood Cemetery was established in 1869 as a burial site for their members. The cemetery is currently owned by a holding company that purchased the back area of the grounds to build a cancer treatment center and reinterred remains in a mass grave in the front corner. There are a series of large tablets bearing the names of those individuals, and some of the original tombstones have been placed in orderly rows just behind.

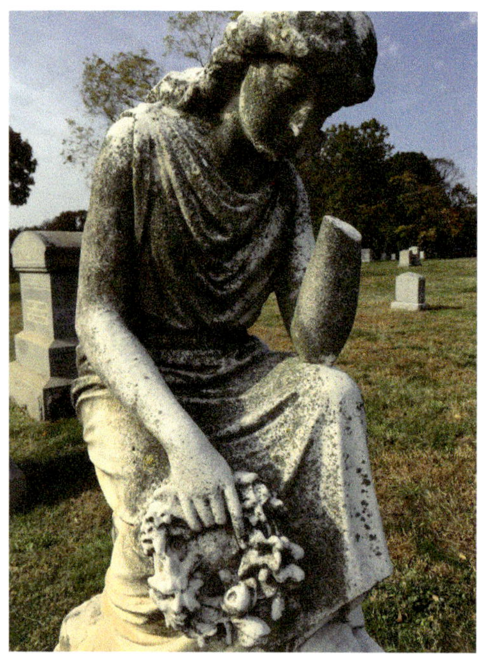

*Left:* Greenwood doesn't have a plethora of larger monuments, though there are a small number of modestly sized statues such as this broken and weathered monument topper.

*Below:* A few places in the cemetery have stacks of iron markers that have been removed from their original locations. One hopes they are being restored and will be returned to their correct grave locations.

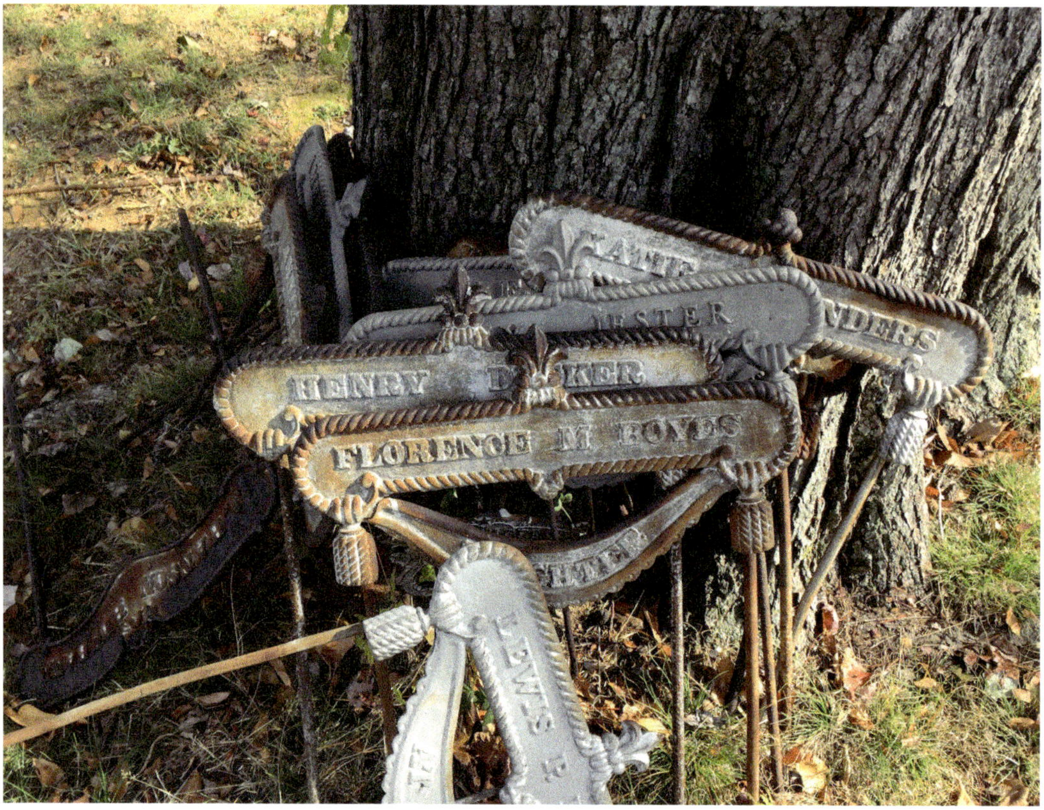

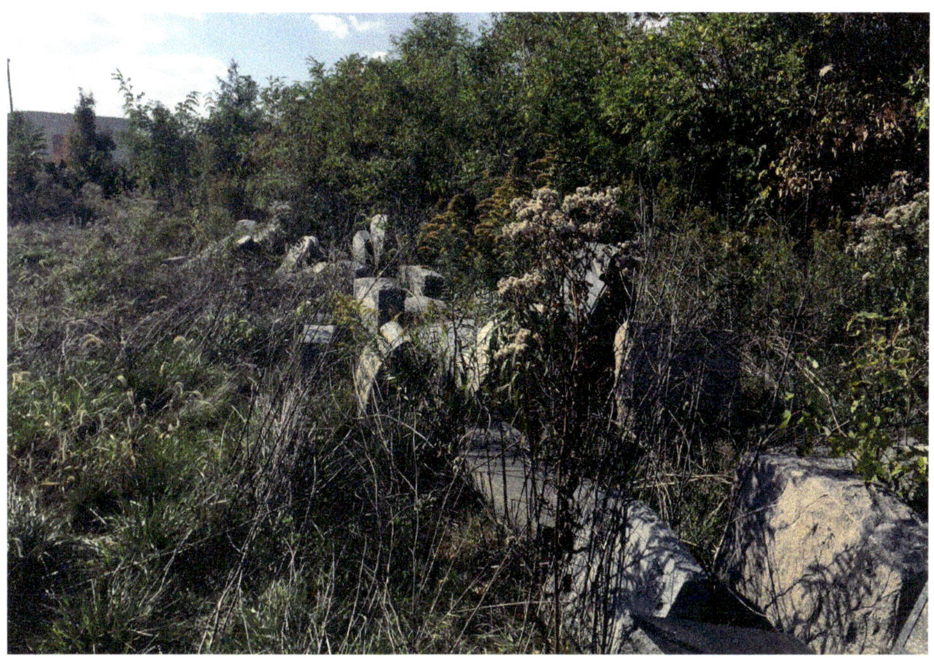

*Above:* Despite a few waves of restoration and beautification of the property over the last ten-to-fifteen years, there are still many areas that haven't seen a mower in a long time.

*Right:* New Cathedral Cemetery sits on the other side of the city from the original or "Old" Cathedral Cemetery. It was established in 1861, less than twenty years later, but it lacks the overall grandeur of its sister site with the exception of a small number of statues, such as this one on top of the Schmitt family monument.

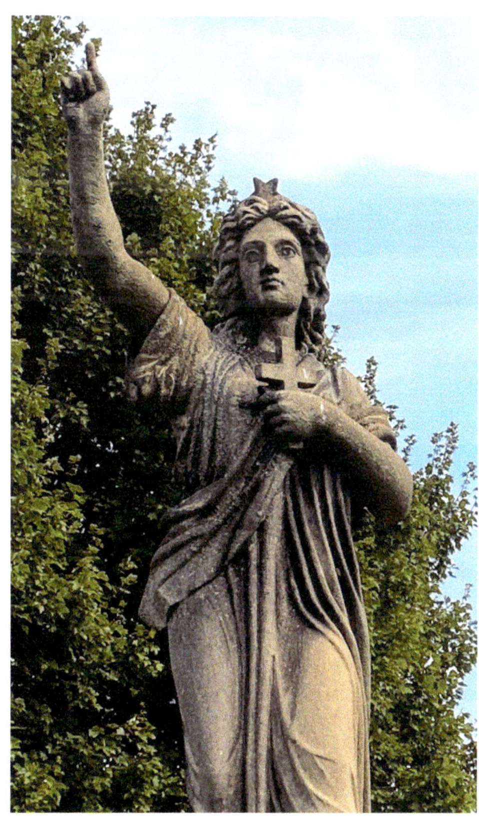

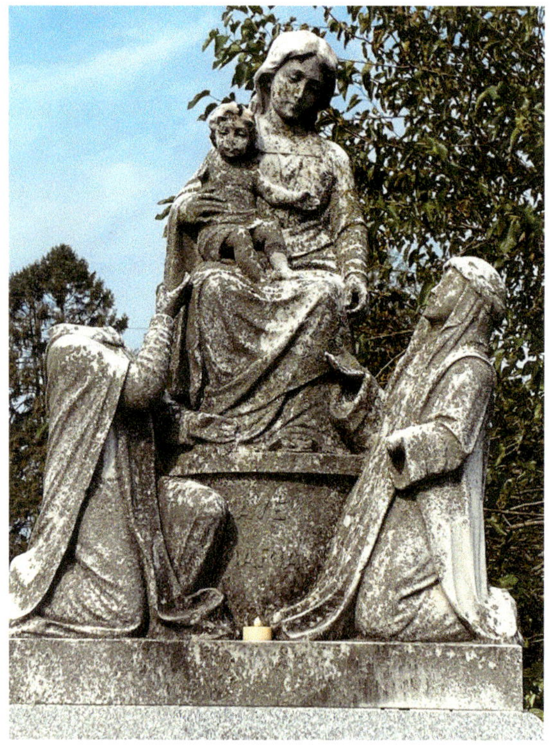

The Madonna and child is a common theme here, although many of these sculptures have seen better days.

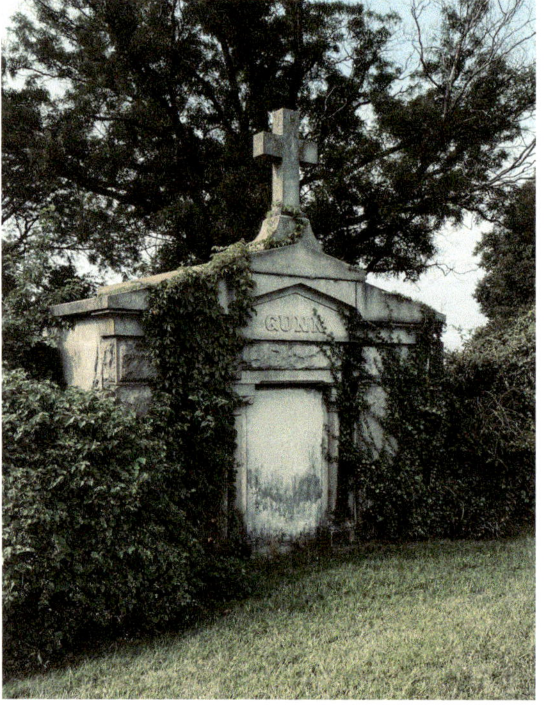

Old Cathedral has a small row of crypts and mausoleums set along a hillside, but unfortunately a number of them had broken doors and gates or were enveloped in vines.

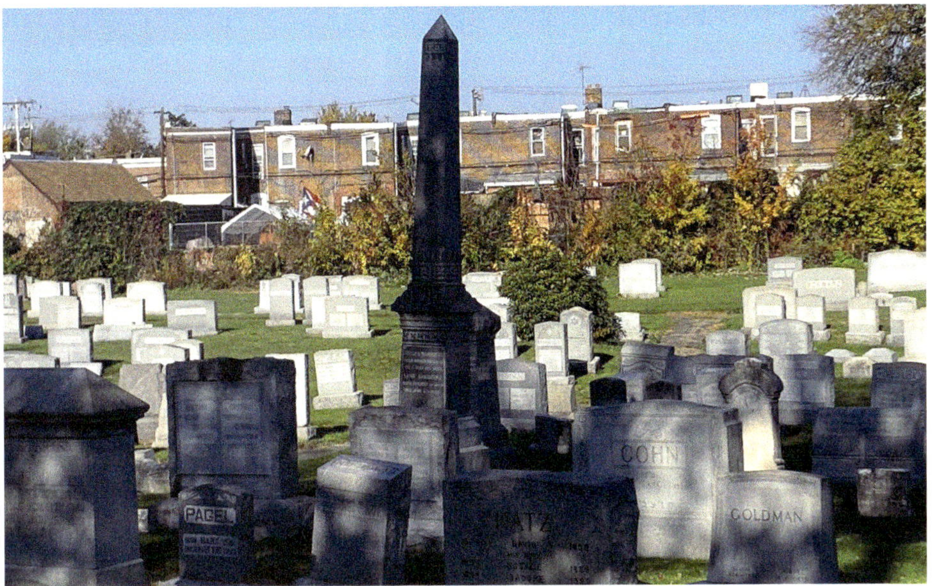

Chevra Bikrum Cholim seems to have been established in the years after Mt. Sinai and Adath Jeshurun. It's a much smaller tract of land directly adjacent to the larger two cemeteries, although set down a step. There's not much information to be found about this tiny Jewish cemetery, and due to its size and proximity to the tree-filled Adath Jeshurun, it quite literally feels like it's in the shadow of its neighbors.

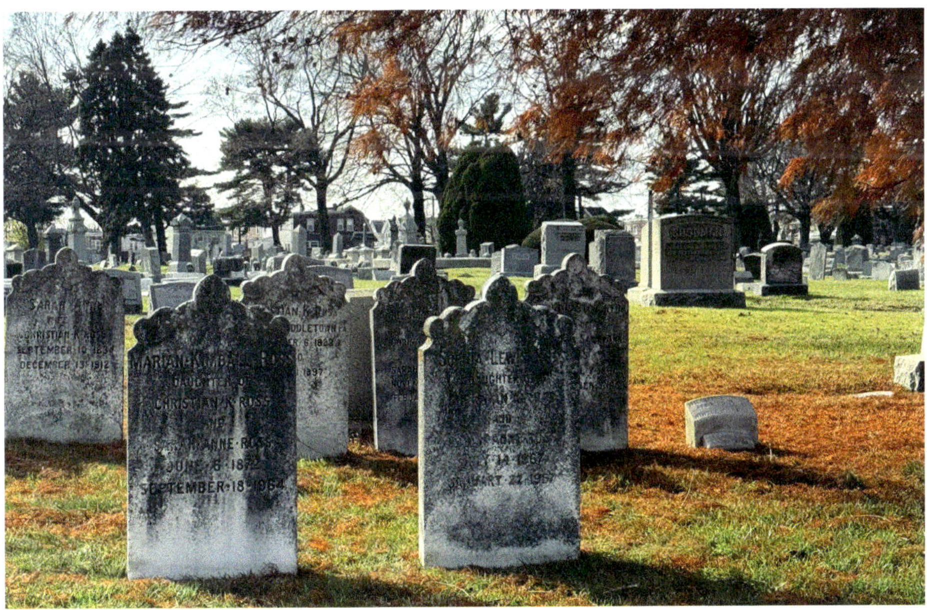

Northwood Cemetery in the West Oak Lane section of Philadelphia was established in 1878 and is still active today. The grounds are fairly well maintained, with some lovely mature trees such as this Bald Cypress with its bright orange fall needles.

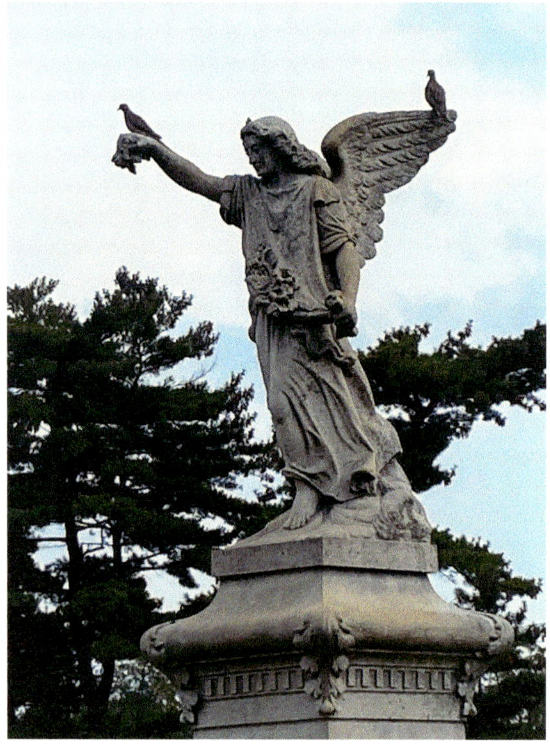

There is less of a detectable landscape or monument design style present here as compared to a rural cemetery. The grounds are dotted with different monument types, from small, slant markers to towering statuary and mausoleums.

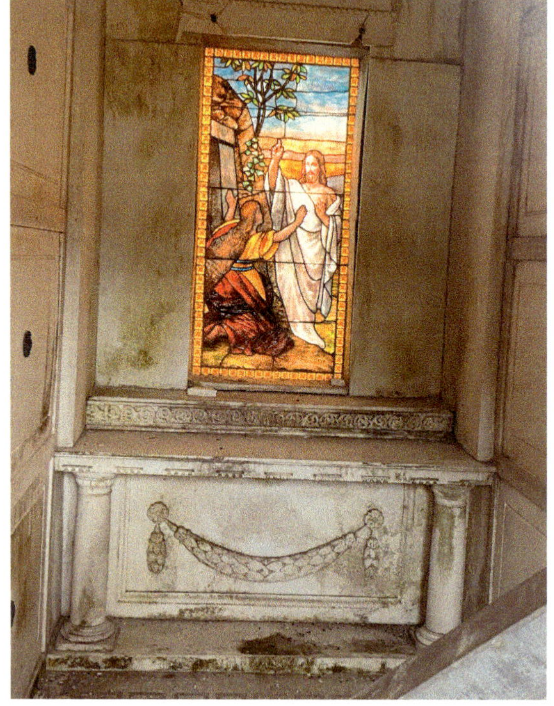

Though it contains less grand mausolea then some of its earlier nineteenth-century counterparts, Northwood does have some fine examples of stained glass; one can tell by the cracked lintel above the window, the separation of stone pieces, and the discoloration on the interior walls that this mausoleum has been greatly affected by settling and the elements over many years.

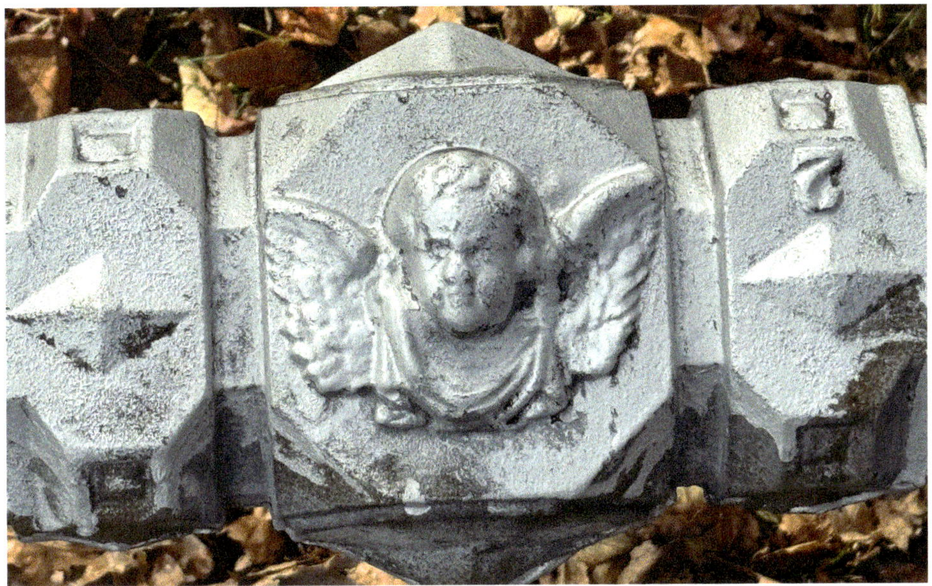

While railings or fencing around family plots used to be quite common, many of Philadelphia's cemeteries only have the stone pillars where these metal pieces were attached left behind. One can still find some of the mass-produced nineteenth and early twentieth-century metal railings at places like Northwood.

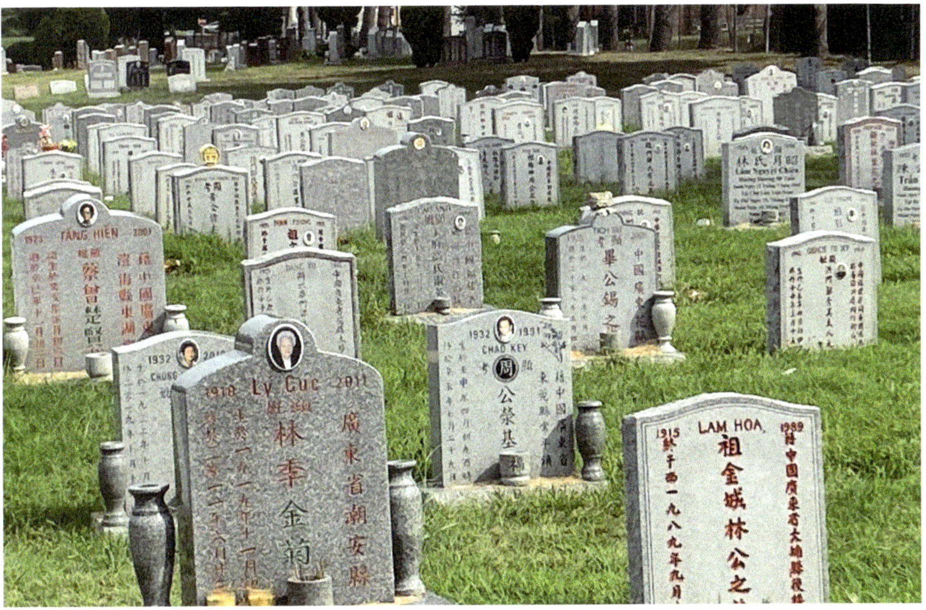

As the cultural and religious makeup of Philadelphia has changed, the styles of monuments and grave decorations have also evolved. This Pennsylvania Chinese Senior Citizens Association section has a lovely paifang memorial arch at the edge and neat rows of headstone with bright red lettering and porcelain portraits of the deceased.

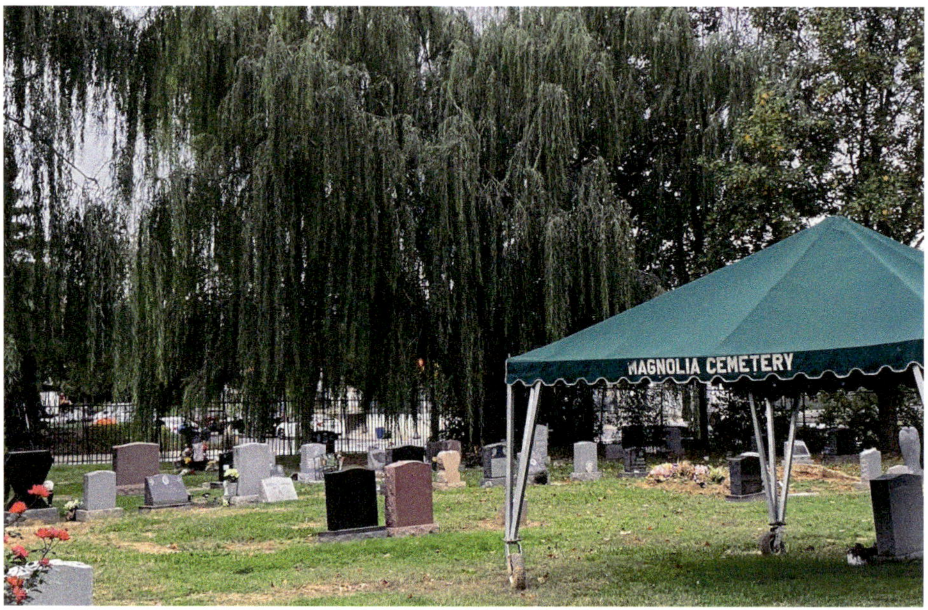


Magnolia Cemetery in the Tacony section of Philadelphia is a small property that seems to be highly active with plenty of room for future burials. It feels like a true community cemetery that represents its locale, and families appear to decorate the graves for every holiday.

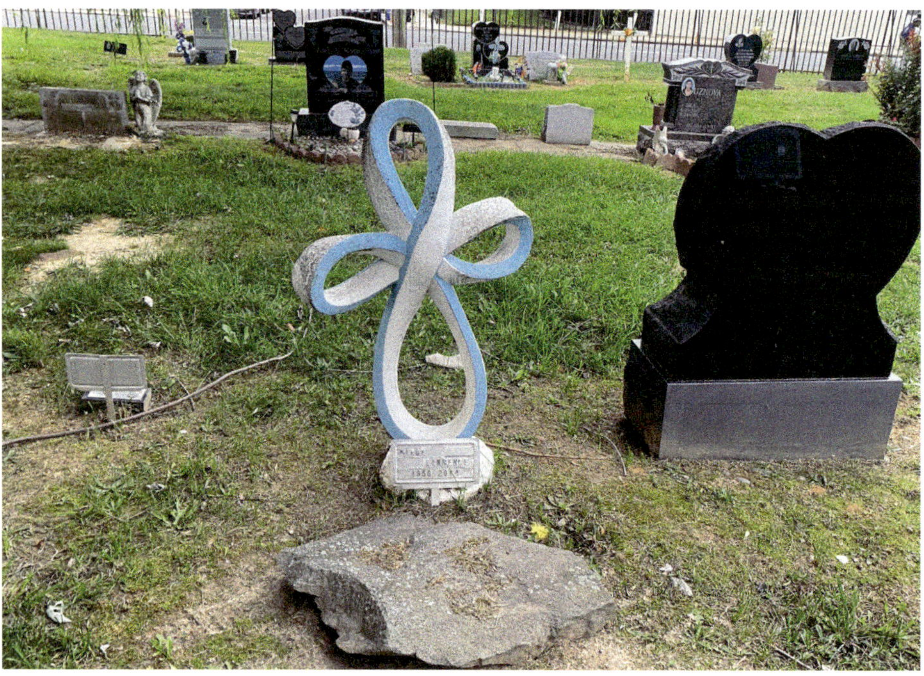

Unique to Magnolia are the number of handmade grave markers, including those created from cement, wood, and even crosses fashioned from PVC fence pieces.

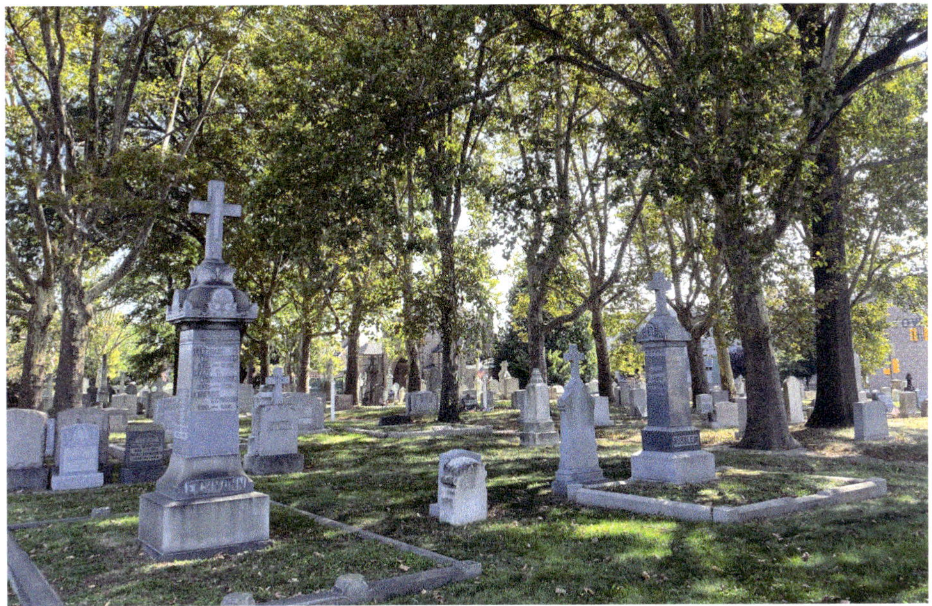

Most Holy Redeemer in the Bridesburg neighborhood was established in 1887 for German Catholics as the Saint Peter's Cemetery in Port Richmond began to fill and additional space was required.

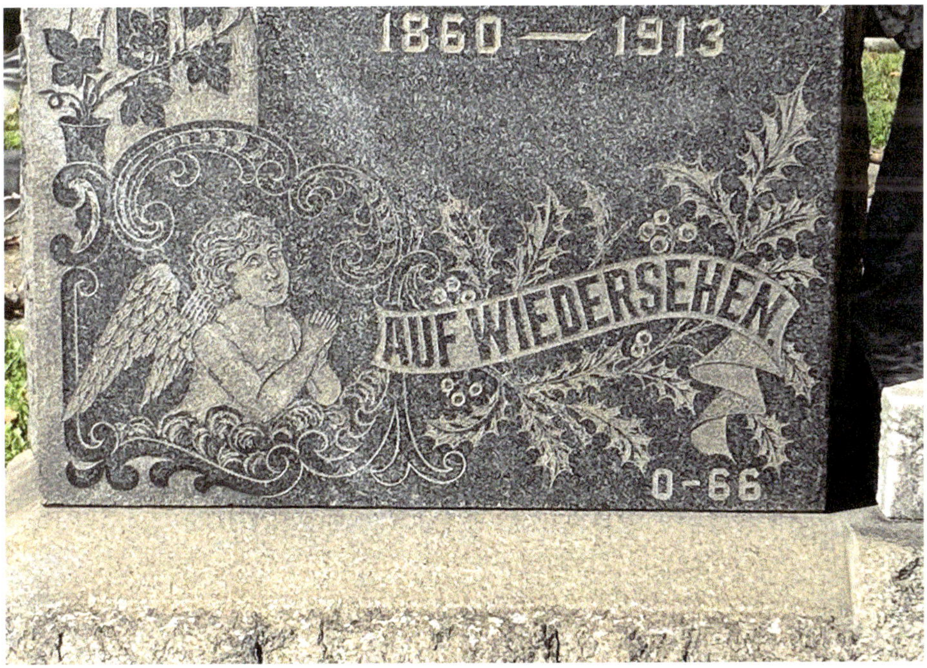



There are many gravestone inscriptions in German, including this early-twentieth-century marker for the Christoph family inscribed with *"auf wiedersehen"* (goodbye).

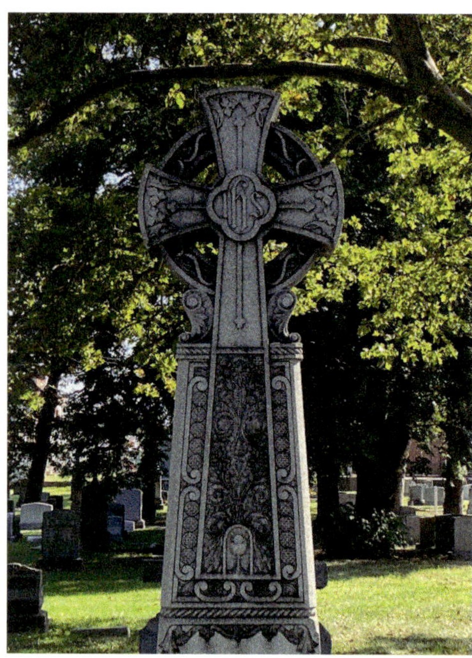

*Left:* It's not clear when the cemetery's population began to shift, but the more modern markers show a change from strictly German Catholics to other Western and Central European Catholics.

*Below:* Some of the beautifully decayed headstones are "sugaring," a term applied to stone that has begun to dissolve and has a granular appearance that looks like sugar.

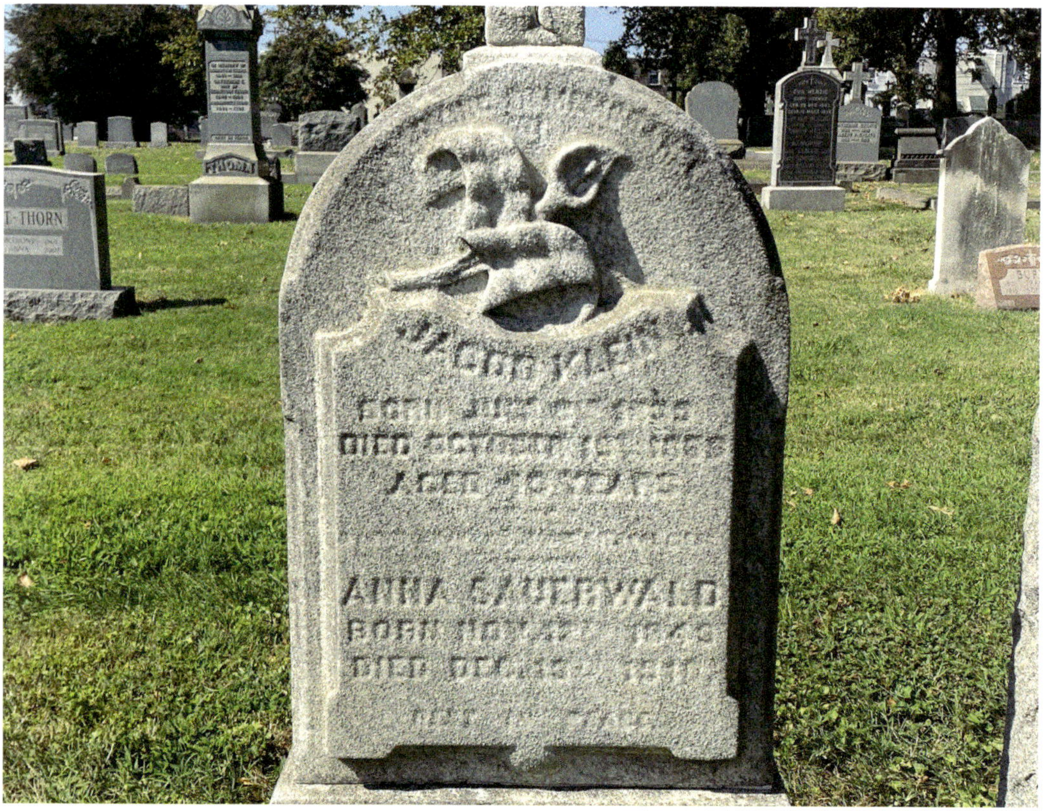

*Right:* Most Holy Redeemer has fine examples of porcelain portraits mounted to the face of a gravestone, like this one for Peter Frohlich who died in 1920. Although there has been a resurgence in popularity of these types of photos in recent years, the older ones often depicted a person on their wedding day, graduation, or confirmation— perhaps the only time they were professionally photographed.

*Below:* Har Nebo is a Jewish cemetery established in 1890 in the Oxford Circle section of Philadelphia that has struggled in recent years with maintenance and upkeep like so many burial grounds. The Jewish Federation of Greater Philadelphia has assisted with volunteer events and the property is experiencing a period of renewal.

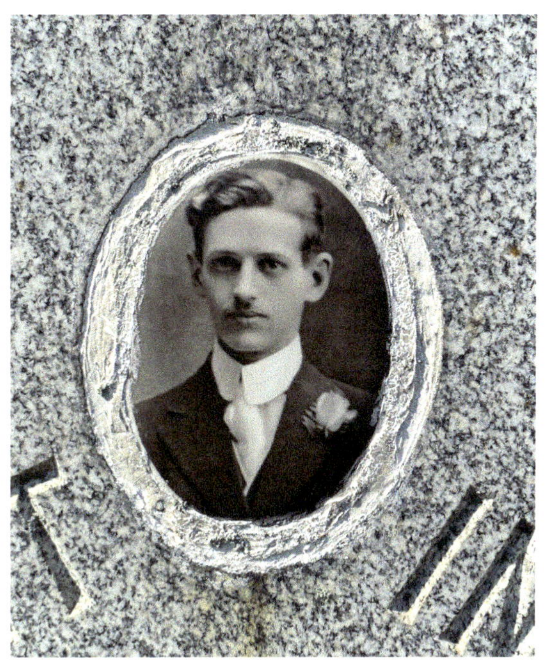

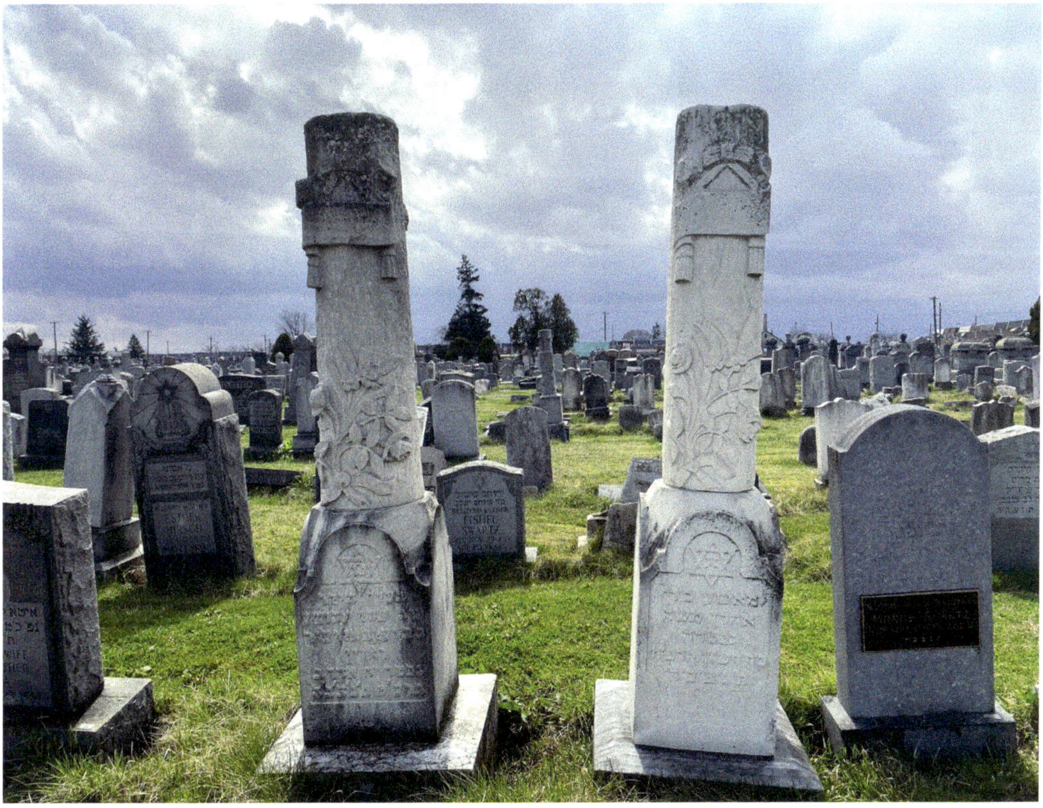

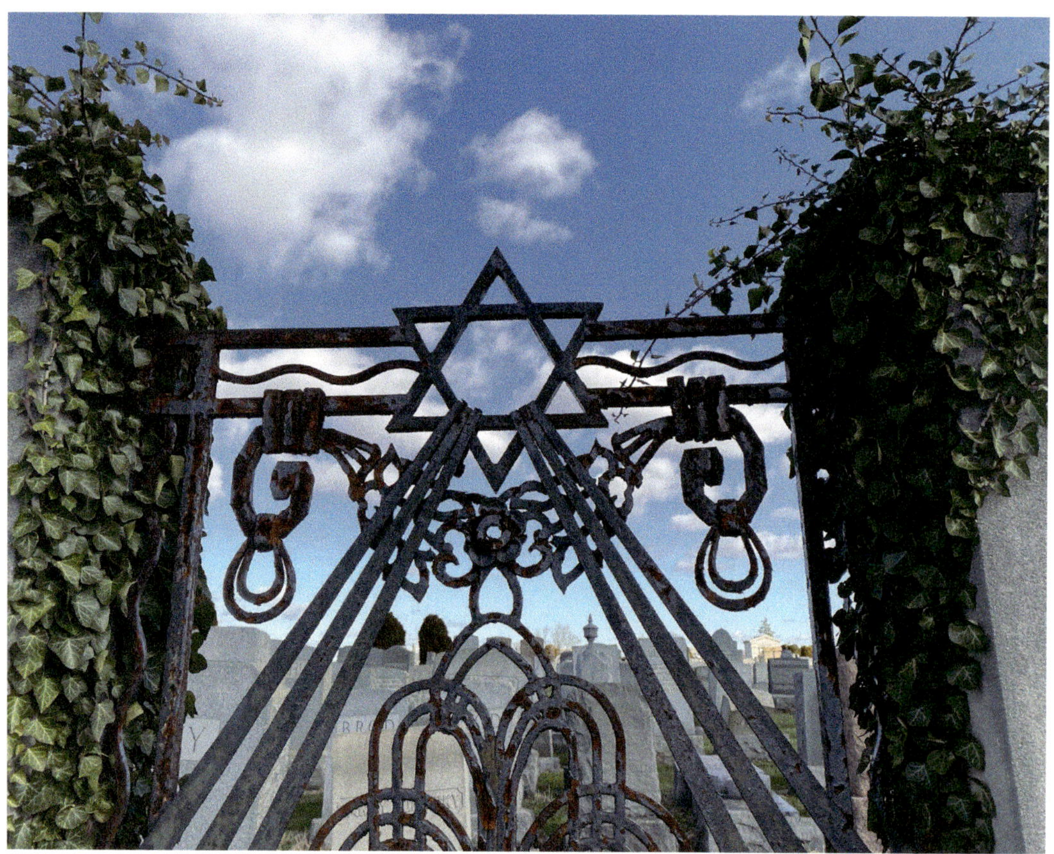

There are a number of gates and entryways at Har Hebo for sections or areas of the cemetery established by beneficial societies. Membership dues covered the grave location, burial, and related services.

# ACKNOWLEDGMENTS

As a taphophile and cemetery volunteer, I spend quite a bit of my free time photographing burial grounds. Despite many years devoted to exploring cemeteries, this book could not have been accomplished without the support and encouragement from my husband, Kyle, or my dear friend, Dani. Thanks also goes to all the cemeteries in Philadelphia, whether fully staffed or supported by volunteers, that are working to keep their gates open and their grounds accessible for everyone to enjoy.

# BIBLIOGRAPHY


adathjeshurun.info
cemeteryco.com
cem.va.gov
findagrave.com
friendsofmountmoriahcemetery.org
ivyhillcemetery.org
kpgreenwoodcemetery.org
laurelhillphl.com
leveringtoncemetery.com
mikvehisrael.org
mostholyredeemercemetery.com
mtsinaicemetery.org
palmercemeteryfishtown.org
pennepackbaptist.org
stjameskingsessing.org
stjamesphila.org
woodlandsphila.org